Scribes in Stilettos

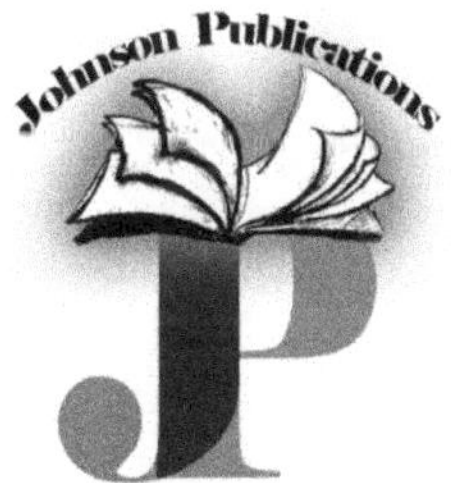

www.JohnsonPublication.biz

This book is a work of fiction. Names, characters, places and incidents either are products of the author's imagination or are used fictitiously. Any resemblance to actual events or locales or persons, living or deceased, is entirely coincidental.

ISBN: 978-0-98404164-0
Published by: Johnson Publications
Newtown Square PA

Cover Art by Syd Redmond of Redsun Media
Cover Layout/Design by Designs by SheShe
Book Layout Design by Designs by Sheshe
Printed in the United States of America

Contact for comments or to order books:
www.johnsonpublications.biz

TABLE OF CONTENTS

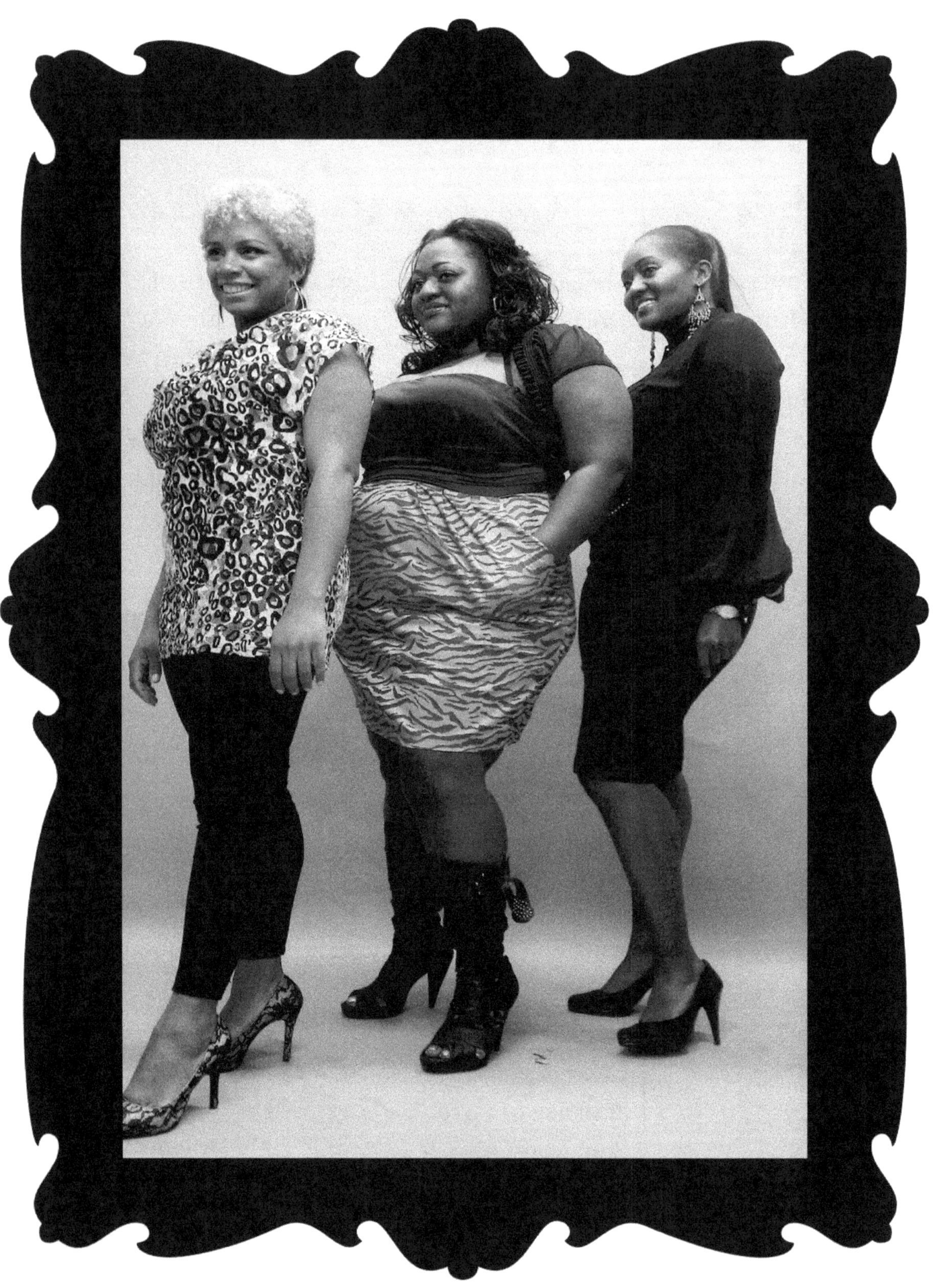

Scribes in Stilettos

Lati`a Johnson

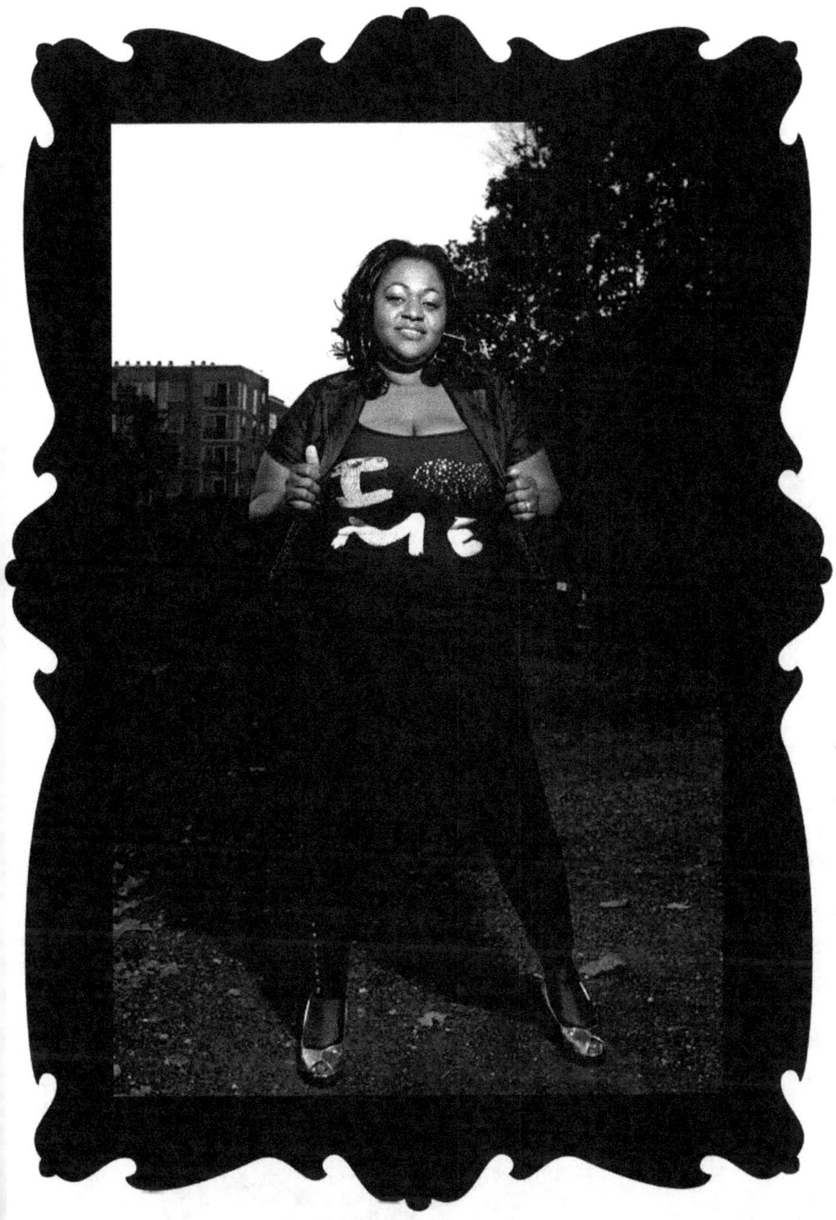

I always knew that I was born for greatness. At least that is what my Momma always told me! Raised in the inner city by a strong black woman with tenacity to go around gave me the strength that I needed to face this mean ole' world! Been placing my stamp on the world since I took my first breath. My life has not always been perfect; but it's been worth it. I take every situation and experience it until I get the lesson. See I found the secret to happiness... and the key to greatness. I EMBRACE ME every second of every day as I appreciate my flaws and embrace my gifts true greatness is born. See my gifts make room for my flaws to become my strengths allowing me to be a lesson for someone else. Welcome to my world! Read as I write my soul...

♥ *LJ*

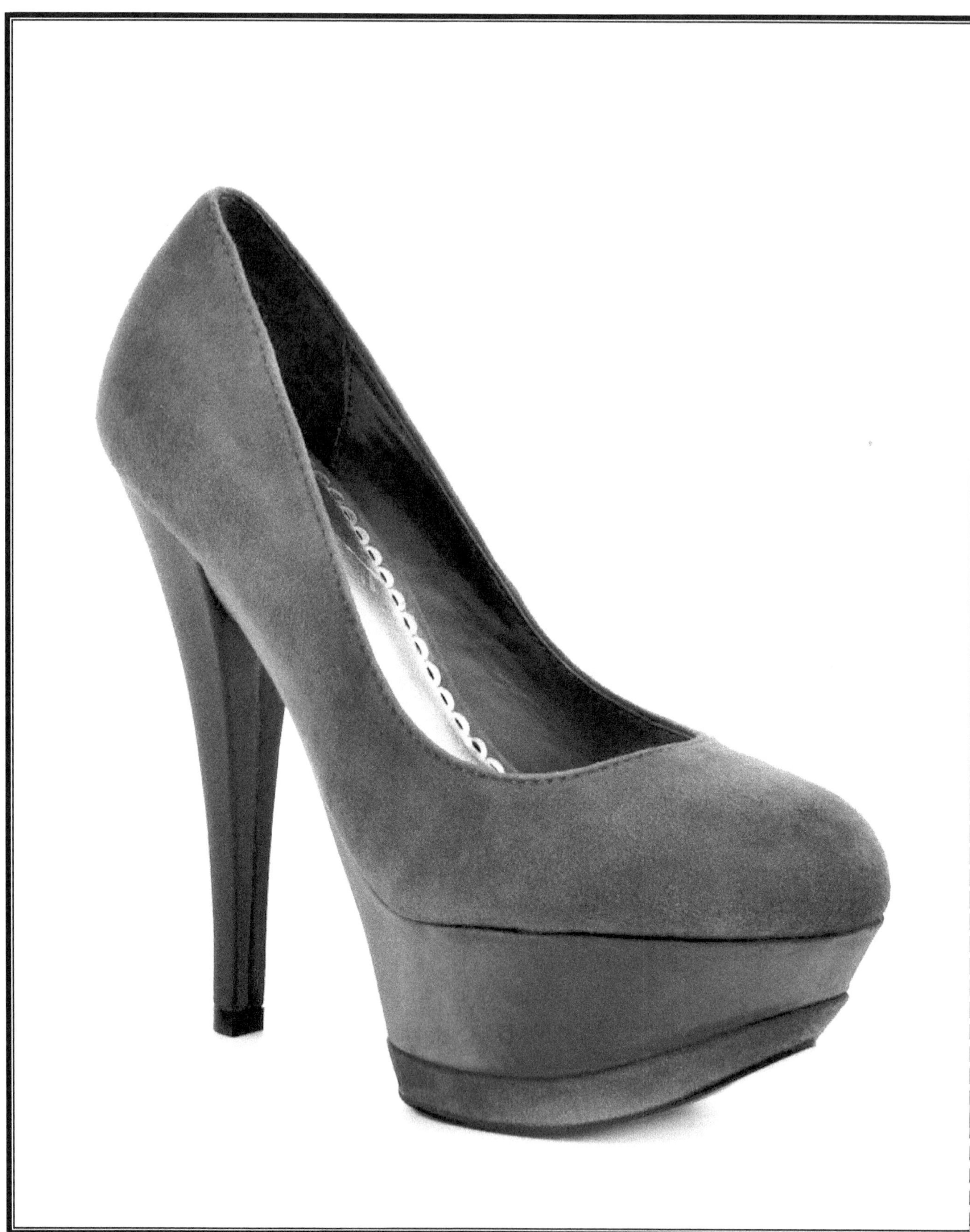

Mind, Body & Soul

Here I am
Transparent
My thoughts being poured upon you like slow, steady
Raindrops
On a Warm spring afternoon
I give it all to you
Freely
Body relaxed
I release words
Deep from within
Words released are
Sacrificial verses of self expression
I surrender my inner thoughts
As each page is filled
With the sweet smell of
My experiences
I invite you
Stroll the halls of my cortex
Experience the warm peace of my soul
Visualize the soft embrace of my body
Take full advantage of this unsolicited voyage
Rest your head on **Love**
Prop your feet up and relish in **Imagination**
Grab hold of **Courage**
Surround yourself in **Knowledge...**
As you witness my
Mind Body & Soul

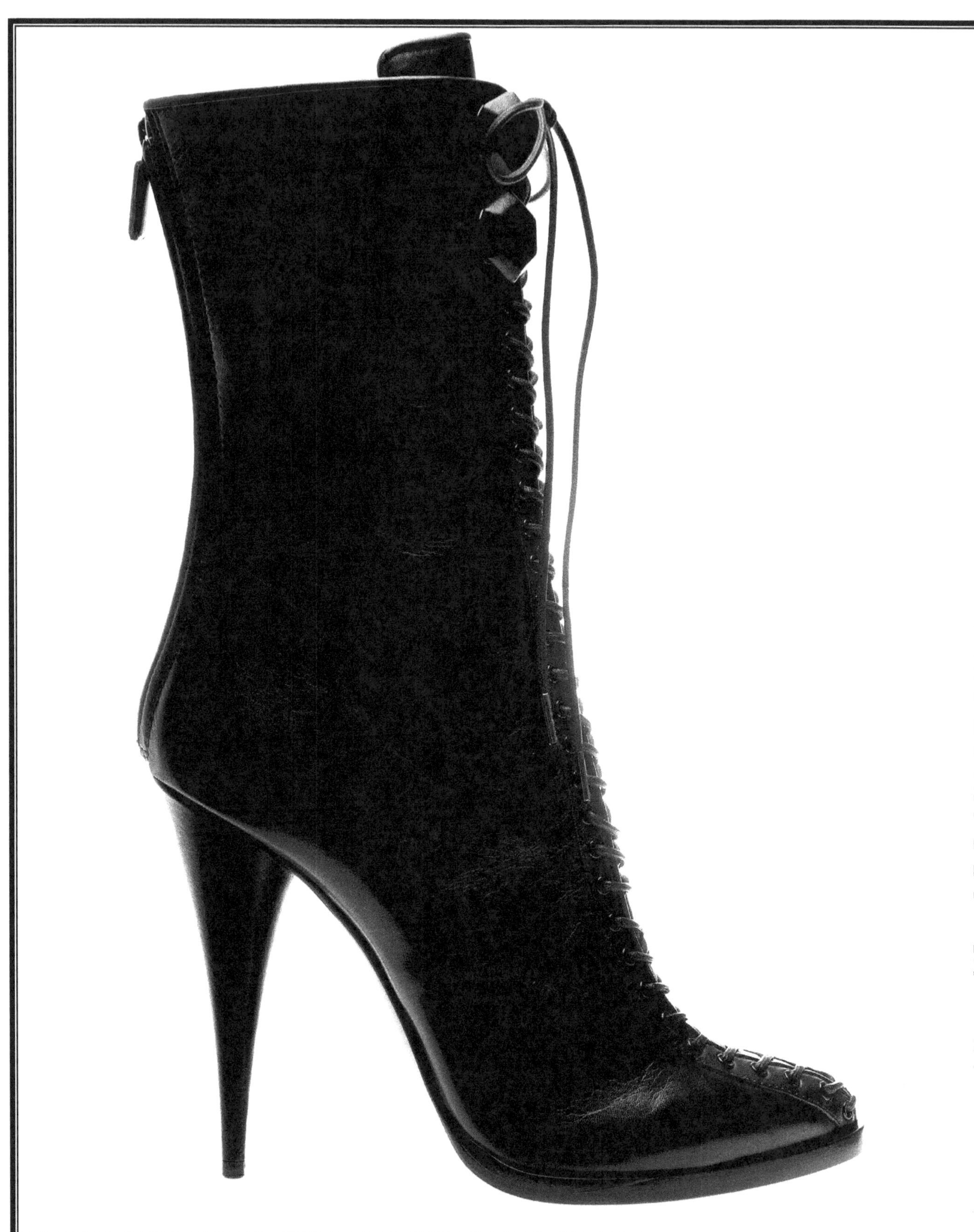

Love and everything in between...

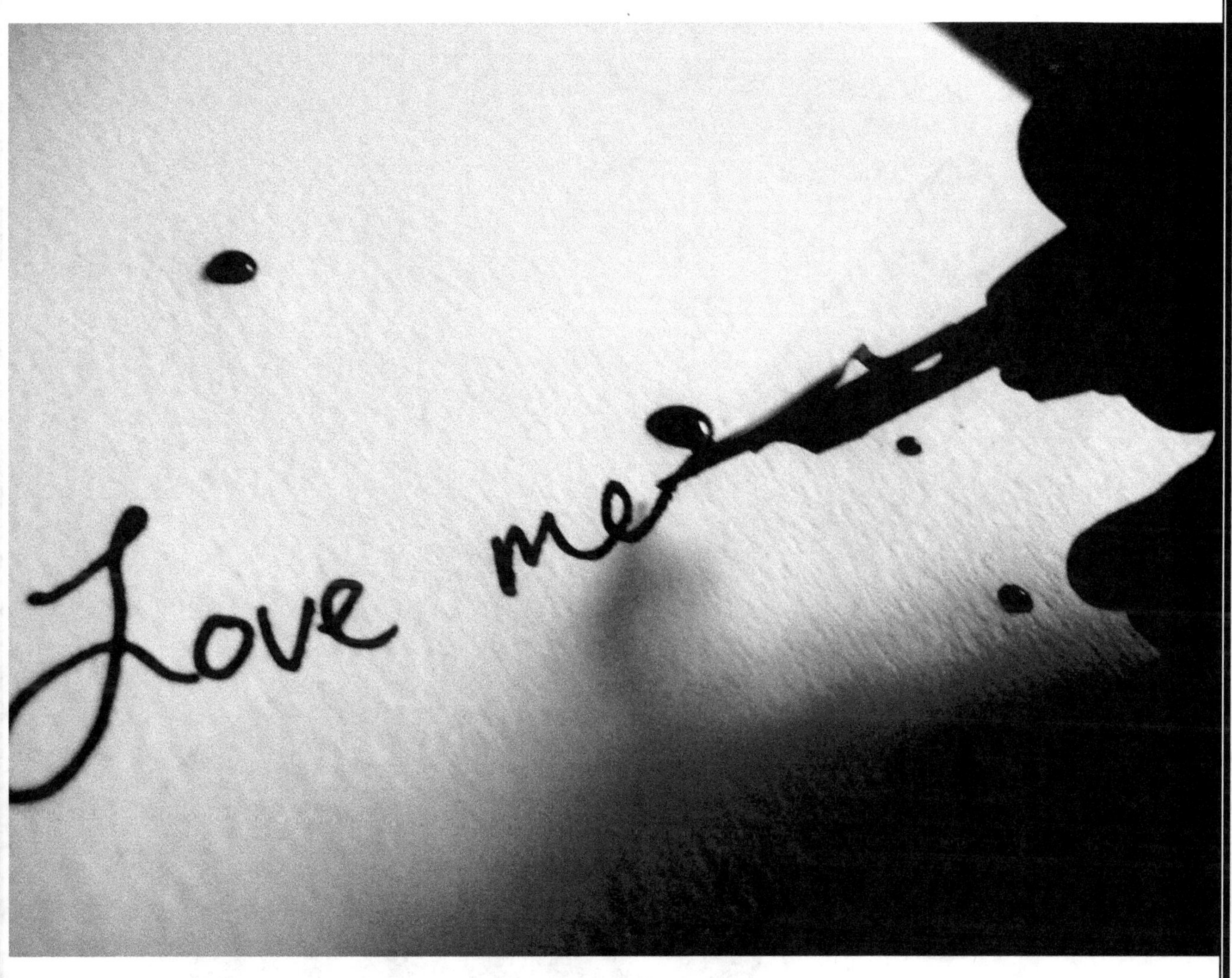

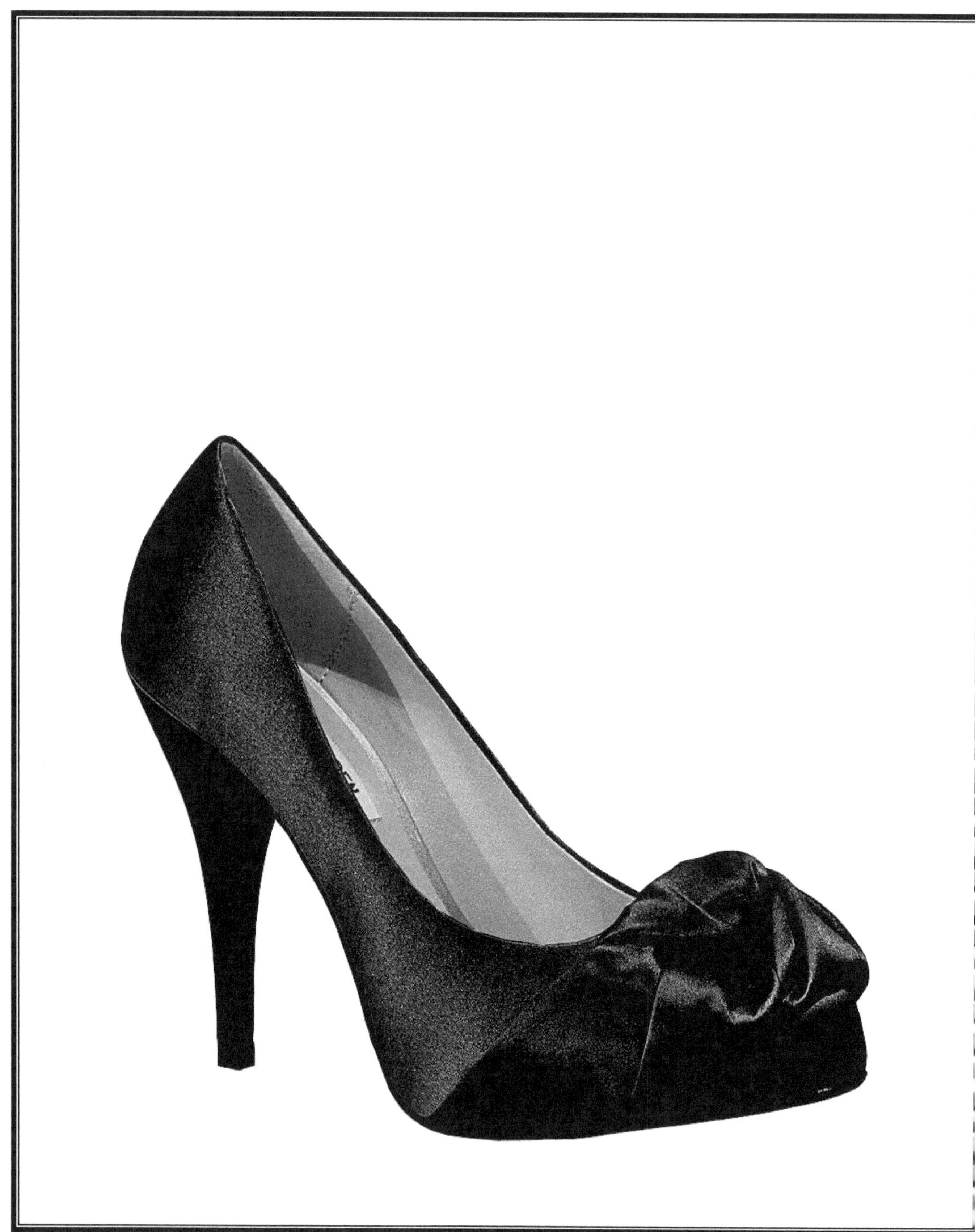

DRESSED UP IN HIM

I loose my composure as I put him on
Every piece of me is dressed up In him
I feel his warm embrace as I light a cinnamon spice candle
Preparing my bath the hairs on my arms stand up from Anticipation of submerging in him
The water warms my body as I feel his essence pouring Over every inch of my soul
I shudder at the thought of releasing his spirit
I stare in amazement as the drain pulls him into its grasp
The bath is done, I'm ready to experience him some more
See I visualize and sense him in all that I do
I wear his love like a pair of soft sexy lace thongs
Close to me and securing my very treasure I share only with him
I wear his smile like a matching lace bra close to my heart Supporting, warming me from the outside in
I garnish my curvaceous body with his kiss as if it was my Favorite,
"Little black dress"
Dressed up in him and loving it!
I admire my threads in the mirror,
Spinning to catch a glimpse of every angle
Knowing that I am truly dressed from head to toe
His love surrounds me, protects me from the harsh Elements of life
His loyalty comforts me, luminous like smooth sensual
Lip gloss as his name escapes
Half parted lips
I stand still a moment in time
I wear nothing but him
I adorn my feet with his touch like a sexy pair of stilettos making me quicken my step and dance all day long
I am dressed up in his essence and wearing him feels so Wonderful

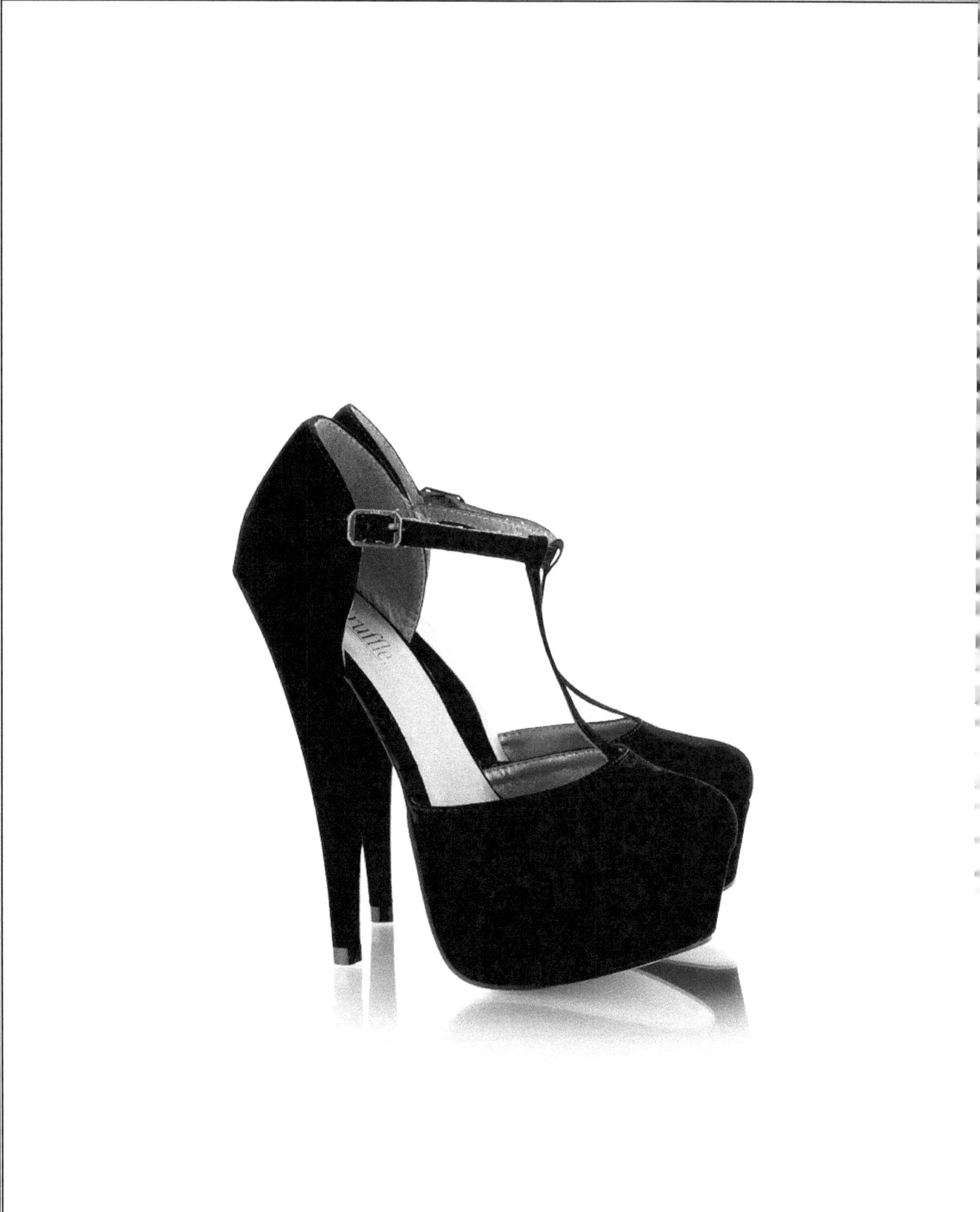

LINGER

You pursued me
Hungry like a tiger yearning for his prey
We stood face to face
Closing a gap in time
Our bodies moved to the same rhythm
The beat slowed as my heart
Beat became faint...
I STAYED TOO LONG
Too long in your grasp
Once warm and electric
Now cold and selfish
I STAYED TOO LONG
Desiring to be yours and only yours
Desire transitioned to lies and resentment
Deep in my belly...
Lingering in your essence
Absorbed in you
I STAYED TOO LONG
I am lost
Not recognized
By the reflection in my mirror
Arms stretched desperately
Grabbing
Searching
For a familiar Image
WE STAYED TOO LONG
Thirsty for the energy in our initial encounter
As we gaze at our sunset...

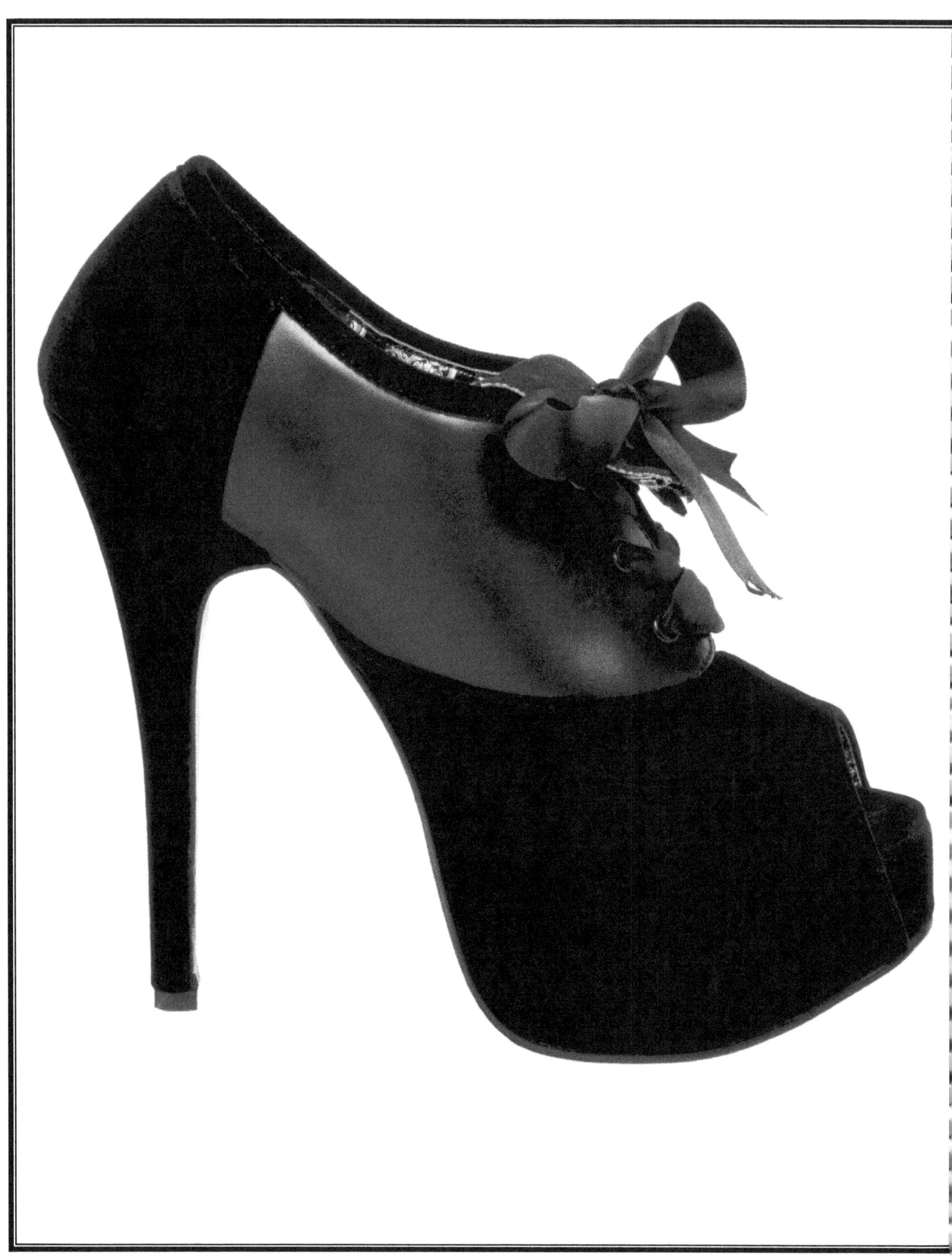

Sovereign Journey

Unfamiliar places welcome my Presence
I freeze at the thought of accepting the
invitation
Turning as I wrestle with
Partial
Exposed face in view
I know you
Our paths has forced us into
Counter-productive existence
I desire to remain where I am
So conversant and comforting
As time press on I know
The destination of our souls
Docked on separate piers
Yet sailing the same seas
Unfamiliar places welcome my presence
I fight and struggle against
The invitation
I boldly turn to
Catch a full glare of your knowing
Face
You have vanished!
Forcing me to be
Ushered into Unfamiliar Places
Accepting Reality

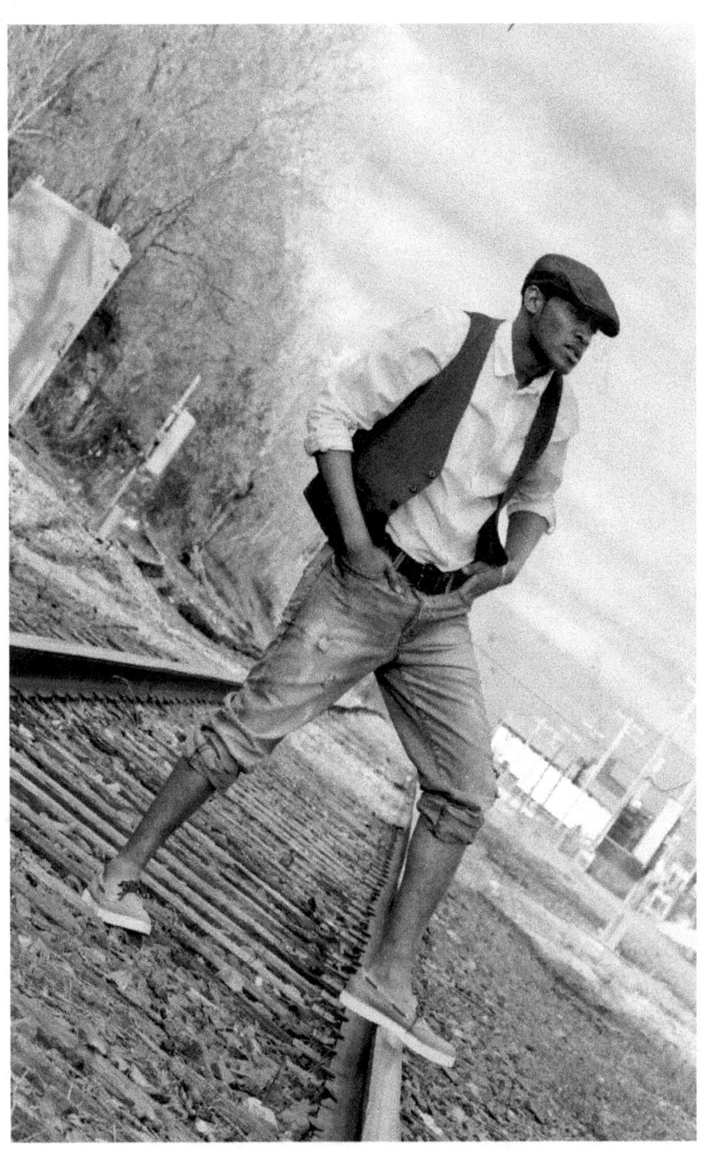

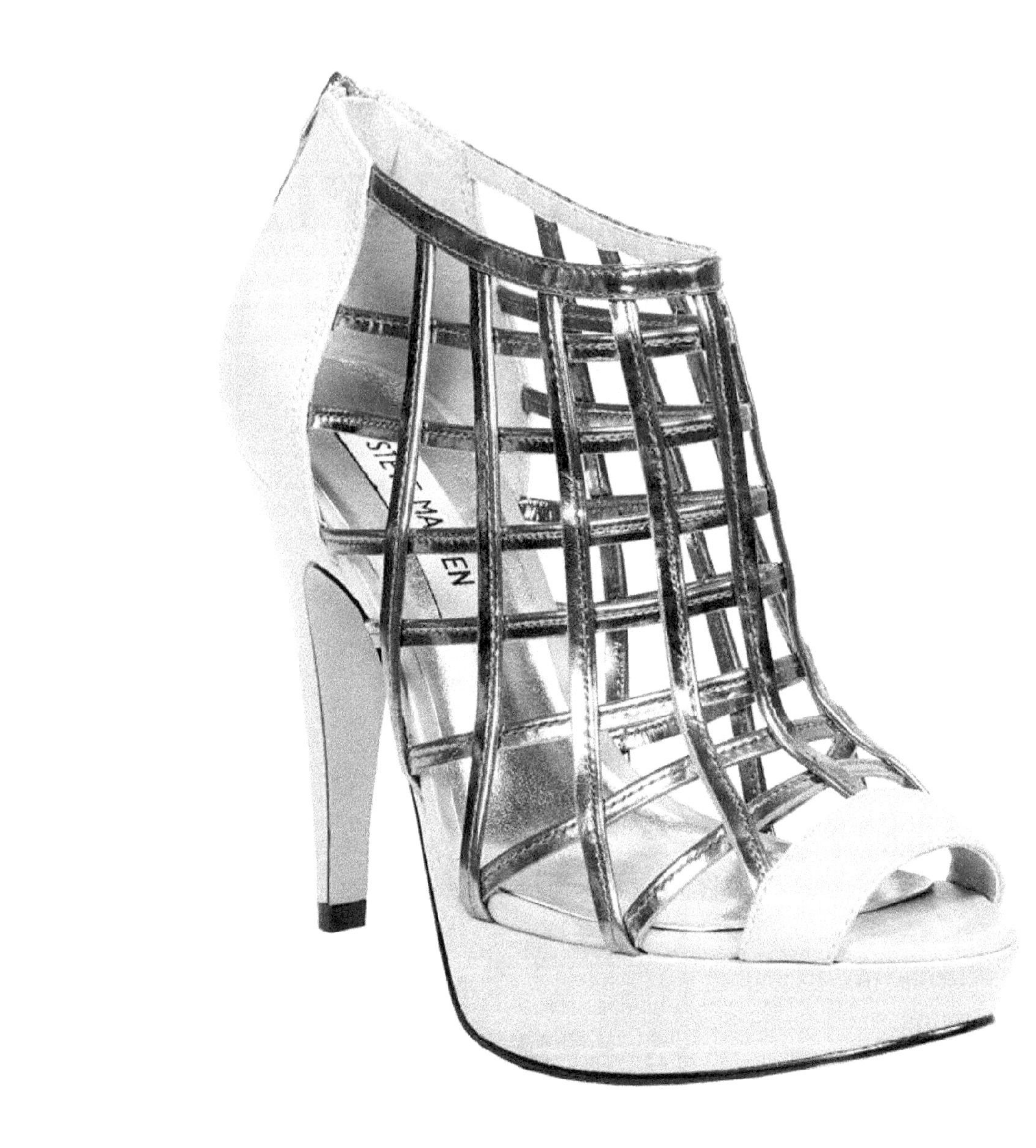

Roaring expression sounds like a trumpet out of the depths of my Soul...

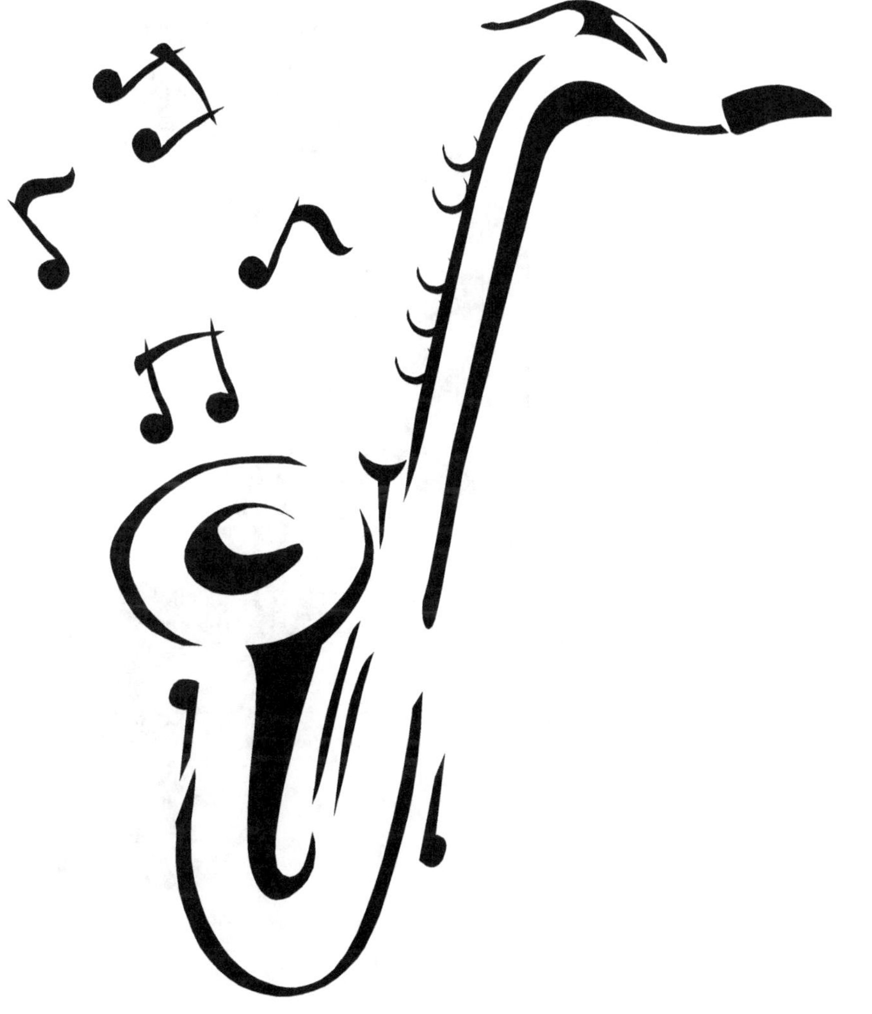

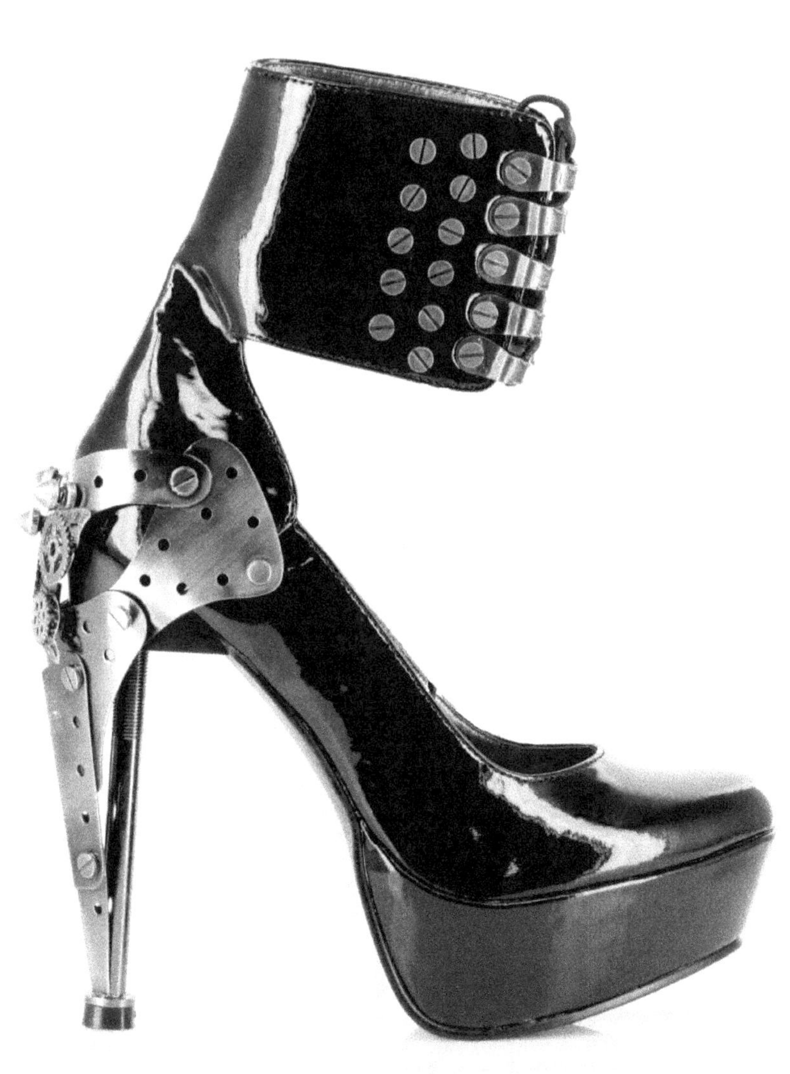

Prisoner of Love

You got me!
My soul cries out to you,
Begging you to free me
I want to be free!
Free to love you and only you
I want to love you all day as we sit hand in hand,
Staring into each other's hearts
You control me
My every thought is of you
I dream sweet dreams of you
You hold me captive even in my slumber
My body is yours
Without a single touch it obeys your command
Your thoughts send gushing rivers between my thighs
I'm yours, your prisoner of love
No shackles needed
Our love connection runs deeper than physical restraints
Our hearts speak the same language
We won't be satisfied with any other
I am your prisoner of love
Insisting that you take me as I am and love me as you will

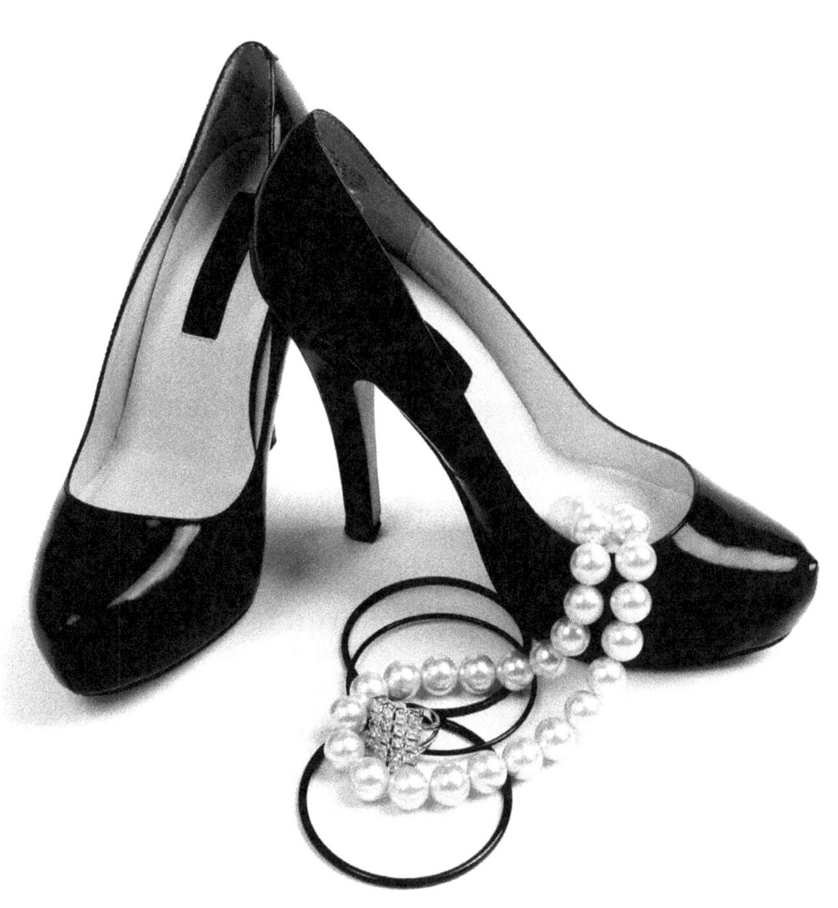

Reflections

In the still of the night,
I catch a glimpse of your silhouette
You bashfully pull me closer to you
Without parting my lips,
I encourage you to be more aggressive
You insist on inviting me in with the subtle hunger in your eyes
Our souls communicate, heartbeat to heartbeat
Breath to breath!
We blend in, liquefying ourselves
Until we appear as one fluid vessel,
Admired by onlookers as a beautiful work of art
They feel the radiance of our union
Lighting the sky like a climatic explosion
In the still of the night
I caught a glimpse of your silhouette
And truly understood love

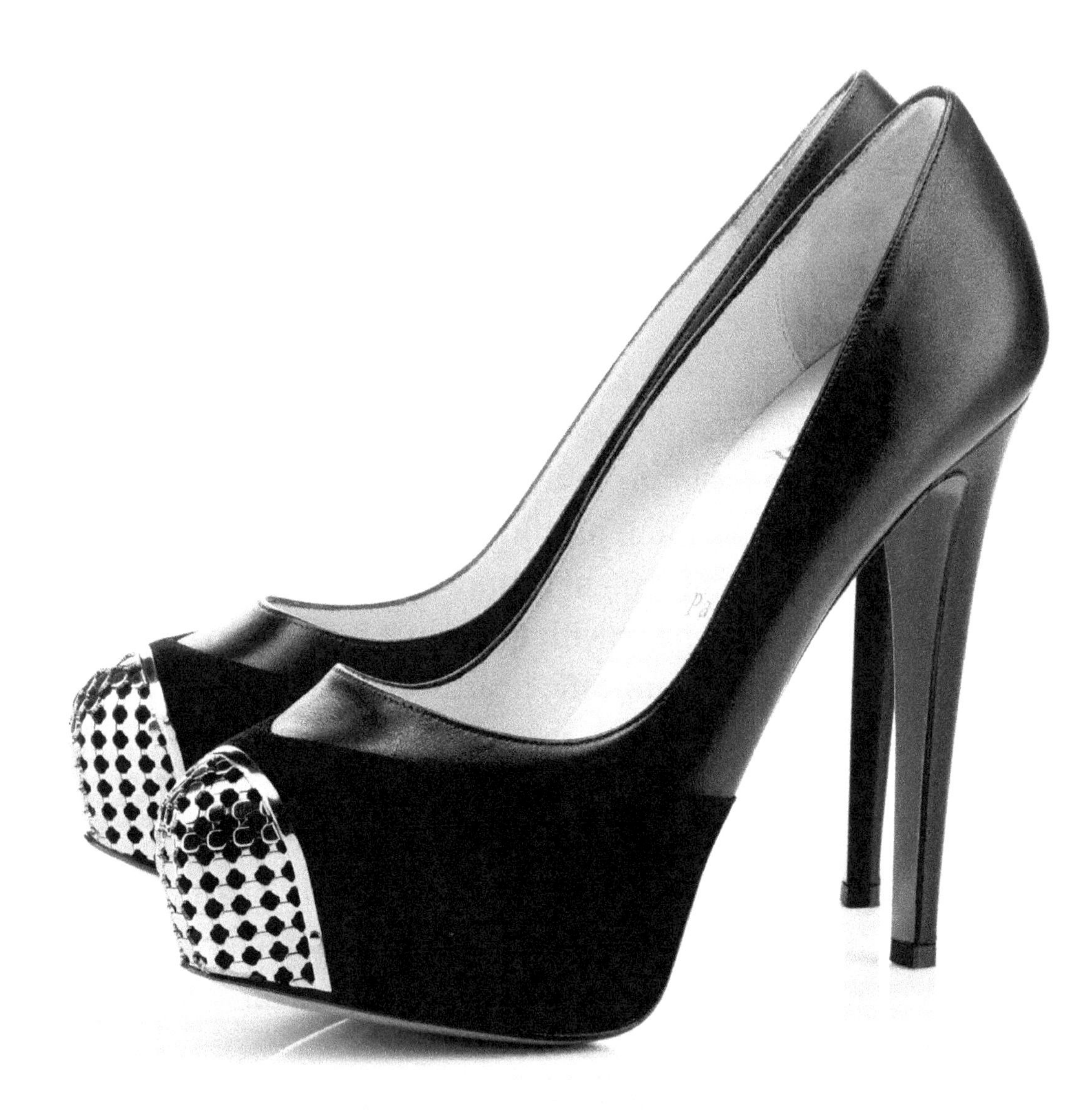

Submerge

Excitement glowing from within
In Your presence
Wanting to know you better
Intrigued by your devilish grin
Your stare draws me closer in
Curiosity heightens
I yearn to reach the depths of your manhood
Fascinated I patiently wait
To master your soul

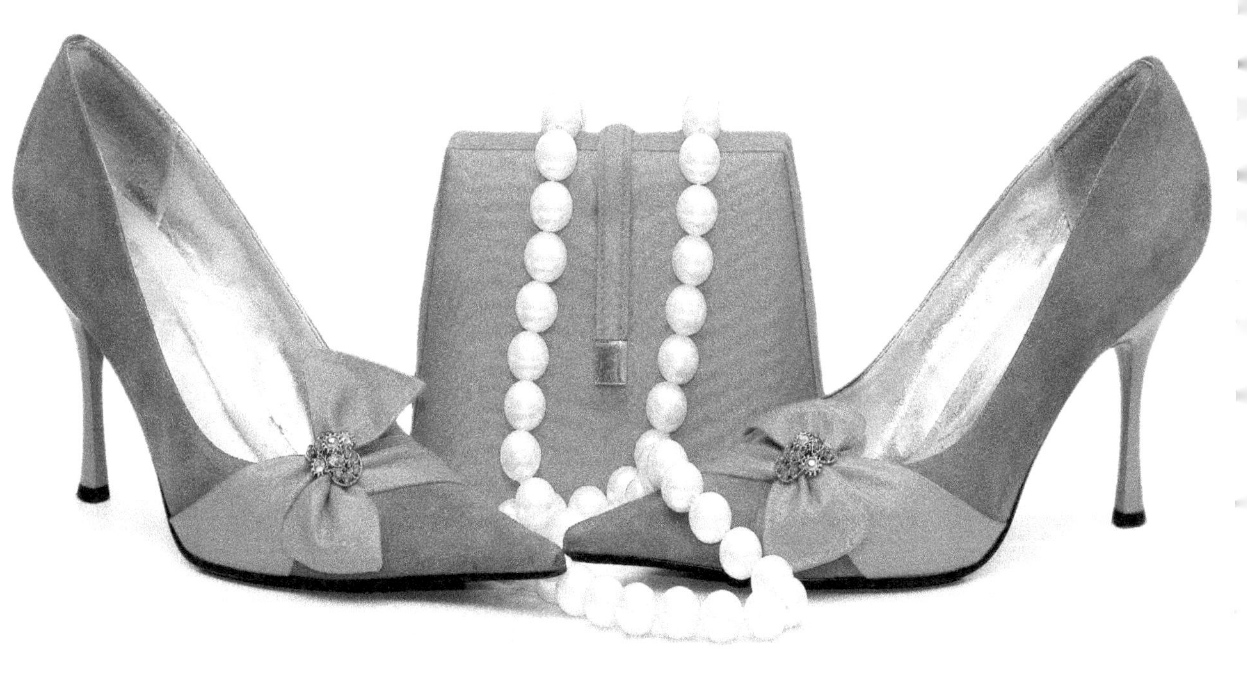

Images they go through my mind breaking through as the sun does at first light...

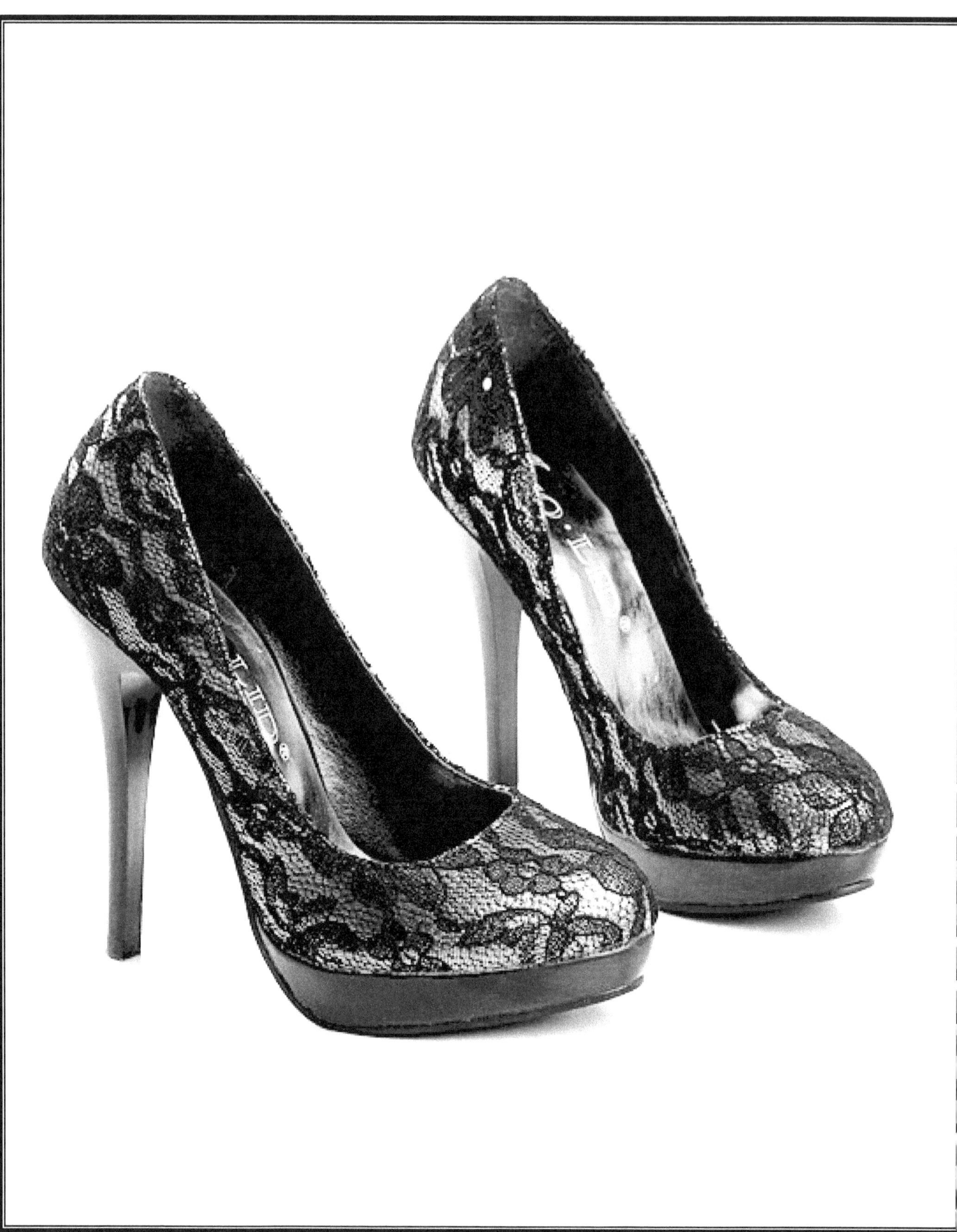

BEQUEST

I am gifted; I mean truly gifted
I possess the ability to express myself
I mean- I am expression!
I have metaphors
Addictive adjectives and vibrating
verbs
Pulsating through my veins
Every beat of my heart pumps
billions of artistic cells
Throughout my being
I will express myself at all times
I will not relinquish my craft to those
who claim to set the bar of excellence
I will CHANT

I will sing
I will RECITE words of Wisdom,
Encouragement,
And, sometimes a little
Bullshit, depending on my Mood!
I am gifted
Blessed abundantly by GOD
My voice will be heard!
I will be felt!
Even in my silence, my expression of
self will reach
Out and telepathically change the
atmosphere!
Yes, I know the magnitude of my gifts
My prayer is that all my people will
embrace their
Unique talents and esteem each other
Stop letting capitalistic society shape
our conscience
To believe what's hot, and what's not!
When my brothers and sisters stand
before me and
Speak words pouring from their
souls,

I will support them I will uplift them

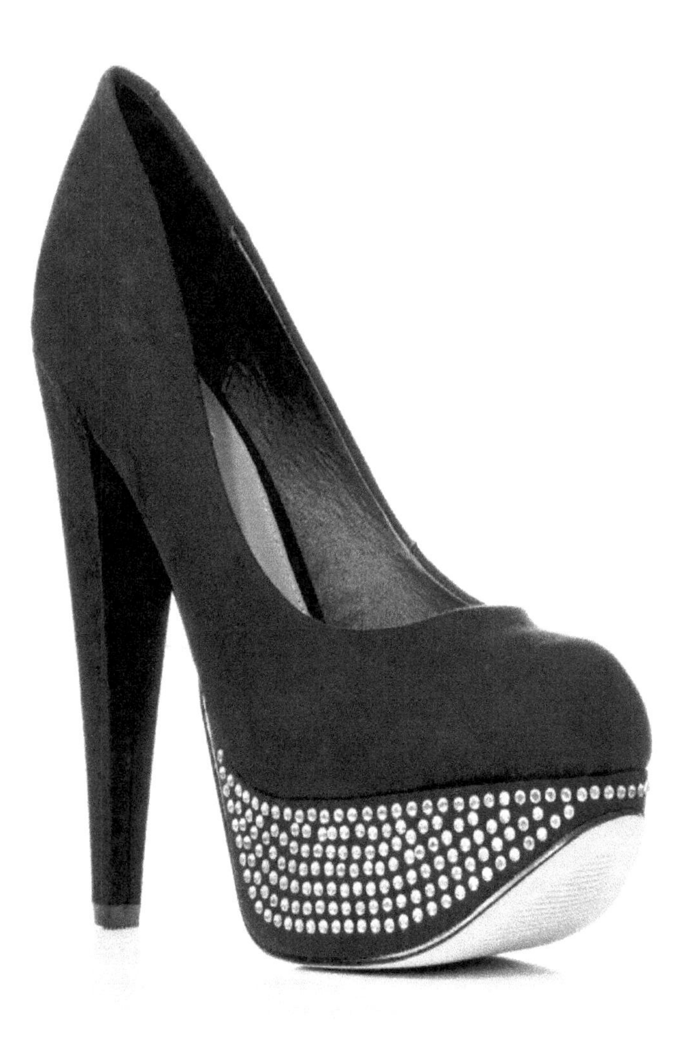

Sweet Sour Love

I captured an image of you in my mind
It left a permanent Ink Stain on my heart
Thinking of your sensual eyes and masculine embrace
Sustains Me
As the moments pass
Days turn into months
Your lingering presence continue to remind me of my lost
Companion of yesterday
I'm forced to move on
Seasons change and the Sun out shine the rain
Yet I remain tortured
Remembering our connection
Is
Bitter Sweet
I can taste the sticky sweet syrup of our intimacy
As the tangy sting of indifference and disconnection
Pierce my Soul
I captured an image of you in my mind and was reminded of the
Ink Stain
That has transformed into
PAIN...

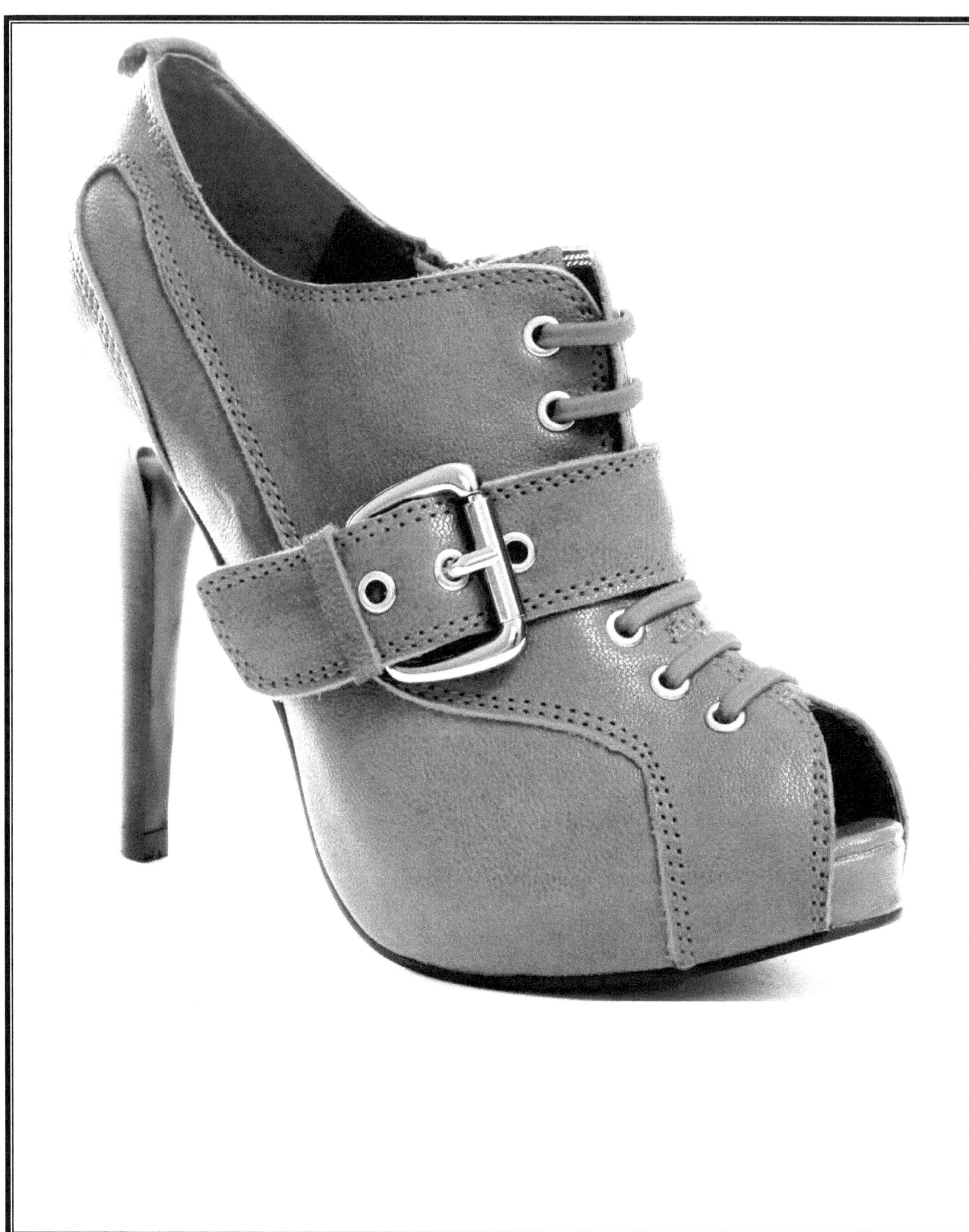

Get Right

Fixated as my eyes
recall your face
Body aching for that
familiar touch
Just the visual of you
brings me to edge of
desire
You're My Get Right
In the middle of the
night my sweet dreams
are you
Controlling my
unconscious
Making me want to
just be
In your space once
more
My Get Right
When the entire world
seems to be against me
Just a slight glance
from your
understanding eyes
Saves me
Supports me
Melts me away
I transform engulfed in
you
You're My Get Right

You hold me close
Dive deep into my sea
Sending waves
crashing at rapid
speeds
My Get It Right
Speechless as you
teach me just what you
hunger for
I labor in love to meet
every request
You're My Get Right
The one I long for even
in your arms
My Get Right
Only you can
Satisfy
Soothe
Quench
This burning deep
inside
I won't be right until
I'm in your presence
Get me right...

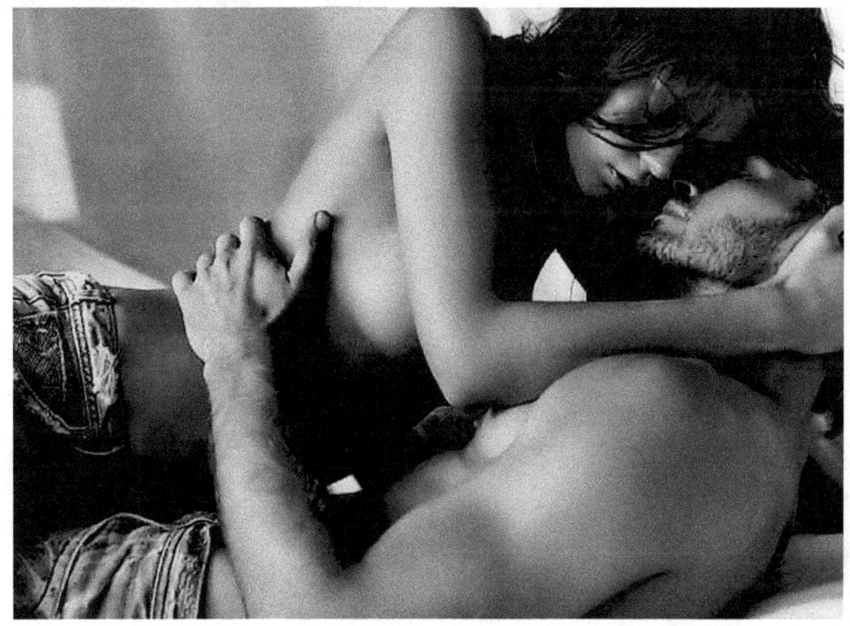

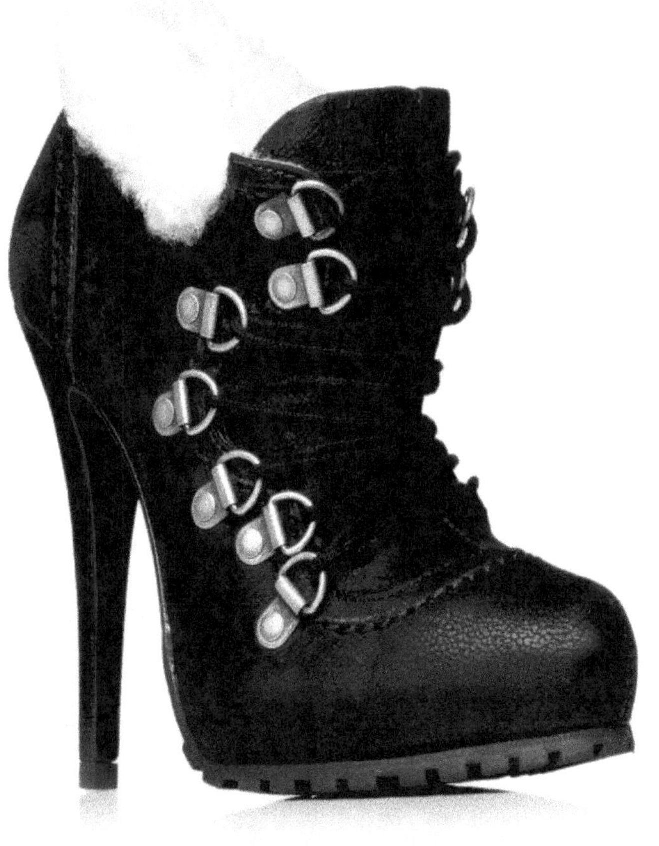

Destiny

Armed with Courage and draped in Confidence
I stand upright stacked on the heels of my predecessors
Strutting, prancing and spinning as the sun reflects its rays
Matching my shine
Armed with Courage and draped in Confidence
I travel the road paved by great women before me
My stilettos adorned with wisdom, humility and self-worth
Evoke clarity necessary for my appointed destination

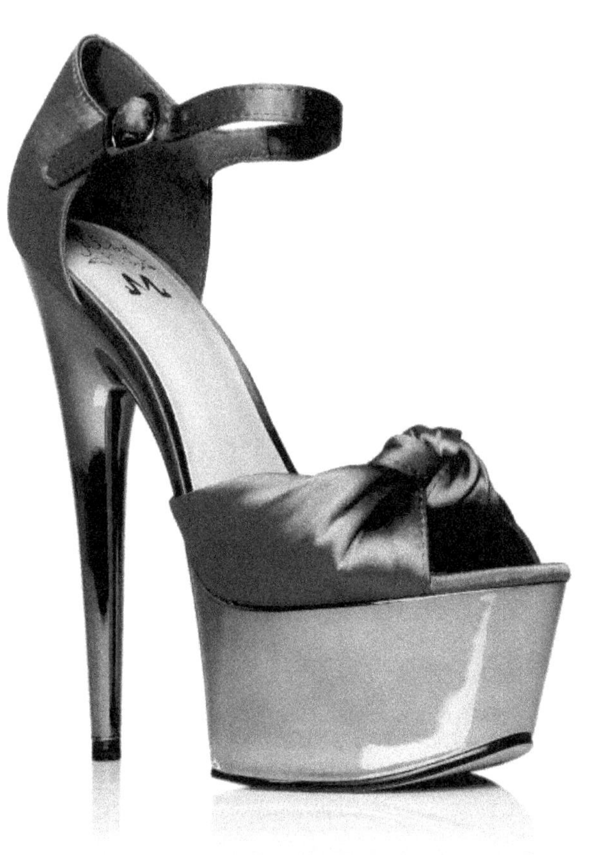

FLOODED

I ran into an old friend today
I saw Him
He saw Me
Ooh there was WE
Sweet aroma of spices
Chocolate and Dripping Brown sugar
Filled the air
Us as a combo sends a syrupy essence of love baking In the atmosphere
Remember the things he would do to me!
Slight touch of our lips sent us both on an exclusive Lover's voyage
Fell pretty hard for him
My heart was Flooded
Engulfed with his quintessence
His wishes were my desires
His smooth choco- skin felt like melting pools of Godiva pouring down on my being
I swear
I swear
It was a solar eclipse with each encounter
Our bodies resembled one complete circle of matter
360 degrees of pure Amour
I'm Flooding
As the memories of our time together fill every
Blood vessel
My heart pumps Him
I saw an old friend today
I was flooded with love
Wonder if he's drowning too

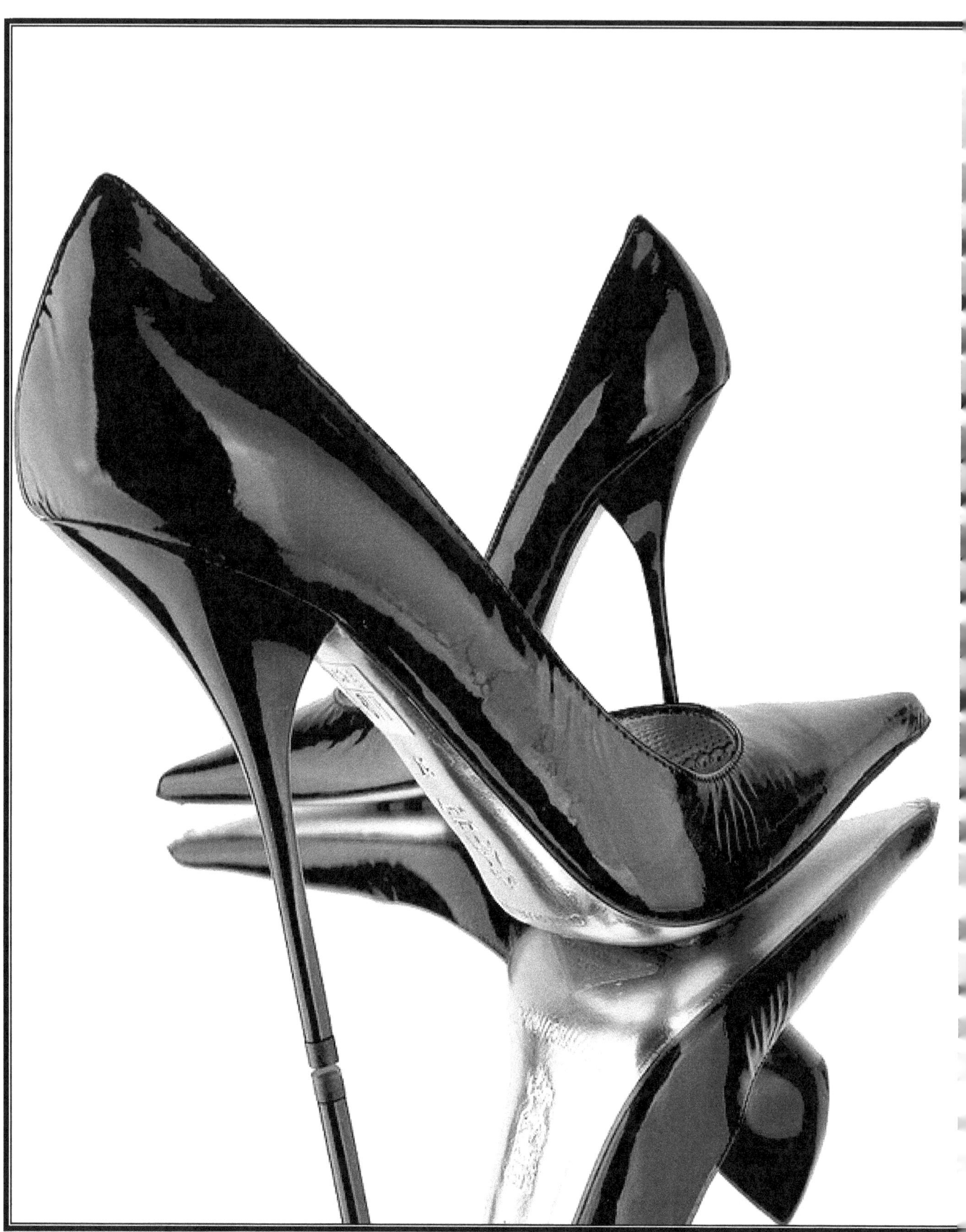

Surely

As sure as love is sent out
Love creates a climatic surge
Touching all that yearn to feel
The presence of...
Pure beauty

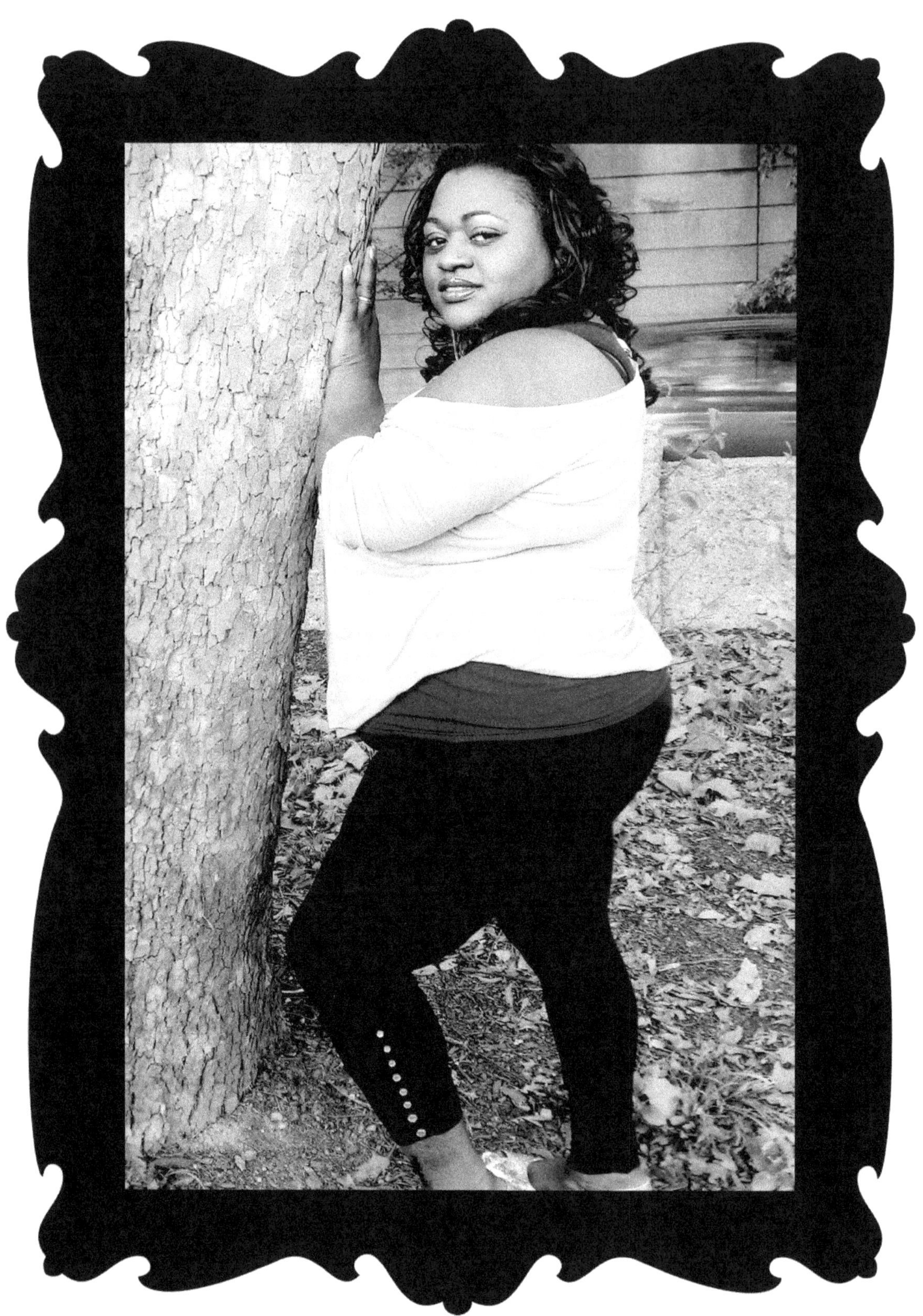

Deep within the treasure of my being hidden away, I offer you a glimpse of my Soul...

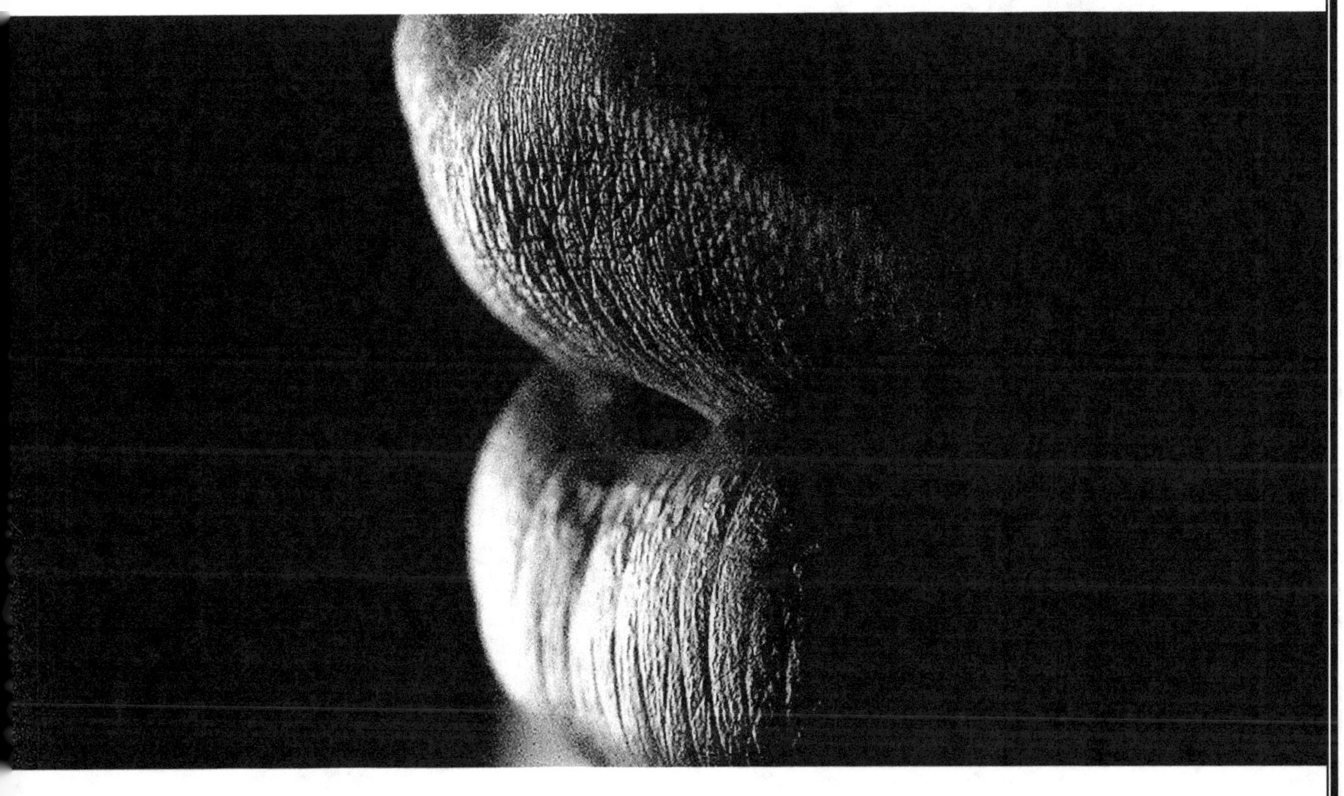

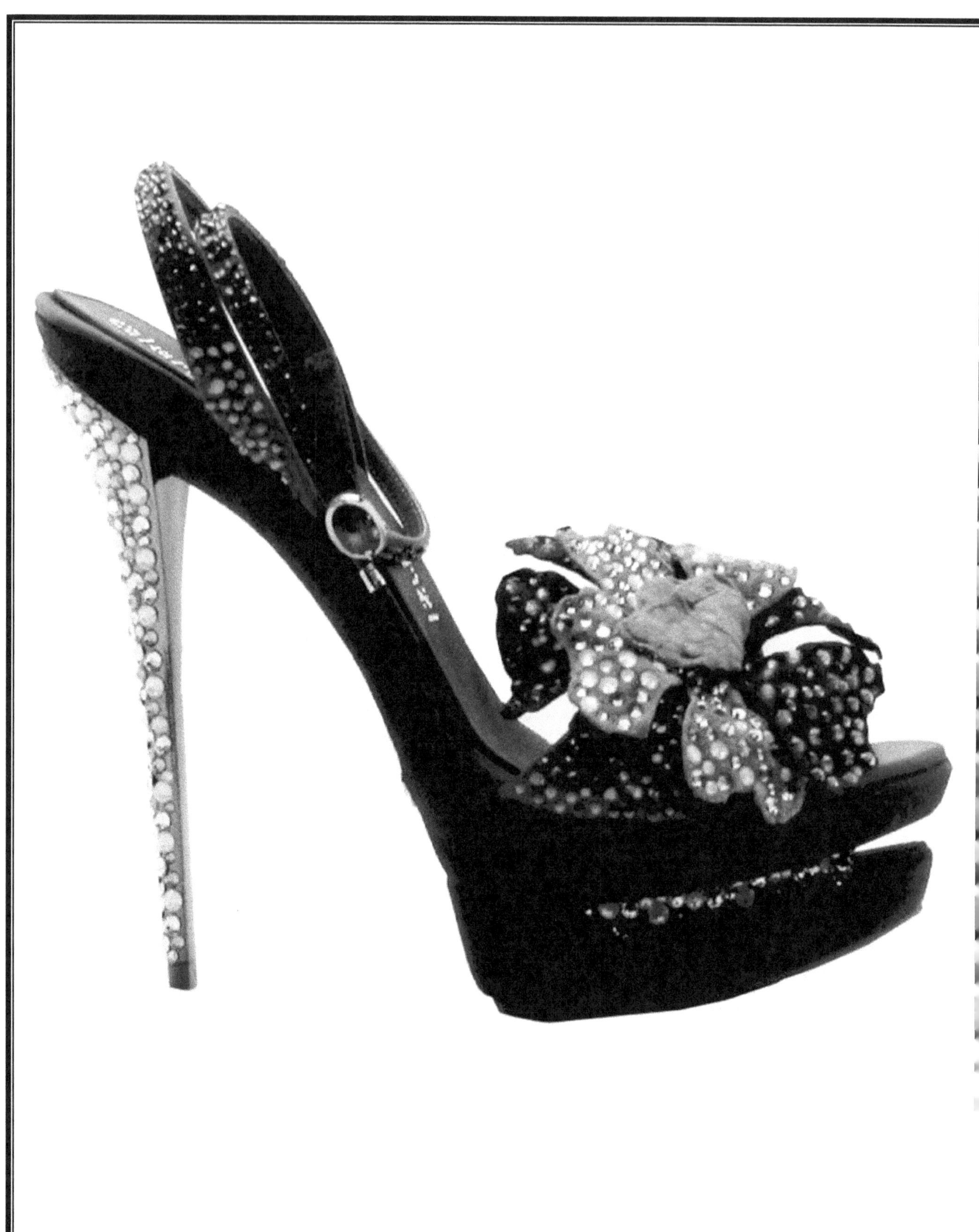

Exhale

Excuse me, I said
Excuse me
Please allow me to be
what
I was purposed for
Allow me to posture
straight up
As my long, thick hair
falls passed the
Nape of my neck
Reminding me that I
am women
Please allow me to
speak words that you
may hear
But may very well may
not understand
The words spoken are
attached to
A lineage of Kings and
Queens
That were deprived of
possessing
Something sacred
That's deeper than the
eye
Can see or
The ear can hear
EXPRESSION!
Yeah, that word just
rolls off of your tongue
Please allow me
To just be
Who I am purposed
To be
My golden bronze hue
May give you
The impression that
I'm just a little less
than you
Don't be fooled by my
humble demeanor
Please allow me to
explain
I am a beautiful hue of
cinnamon
My skin glows like I
was basted in the
Suns glory
My hips are
substantial and I
Possess curves
That swivel and sway
Like a hissing snake
I am fully aware of my
value
Please allow me to be
exactly
Where I am purposed
to be
Nurturing and sharing
encouraging words of
wisdom
And self-worth to my
followers
Please allow me to be
Exactly what I am
The ancestor of those
Strong, deep leaders
That carried the
burden of
Being
Too dark
Too deep and
Misunderstood
Please allow me to
BREATHE!

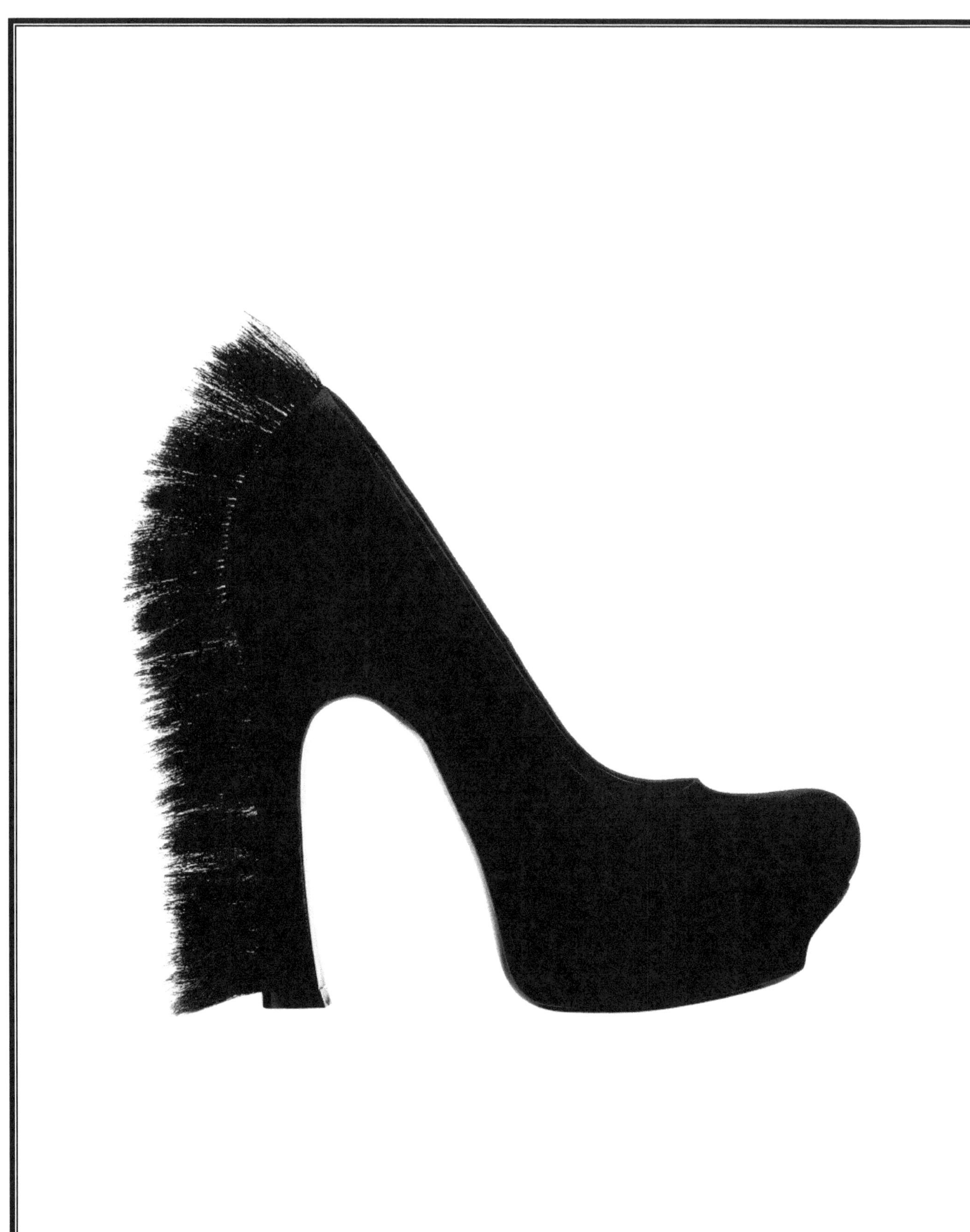

Time

Hello old friend have not felt you in a while
I looked up toward the sun and its' flicker made me
Think of you...
The corners of my mouth competed with gravity as I
Released a bright smile
Hello old friend hope all is well
Remembering how our connection made miles melt
Away like the snow in early spring...
Hello old friend
Waiting to seize one moment in time where nothing
Matters but the familiar thoughts we share
Good bye time missed...My friend will occupy your Space!

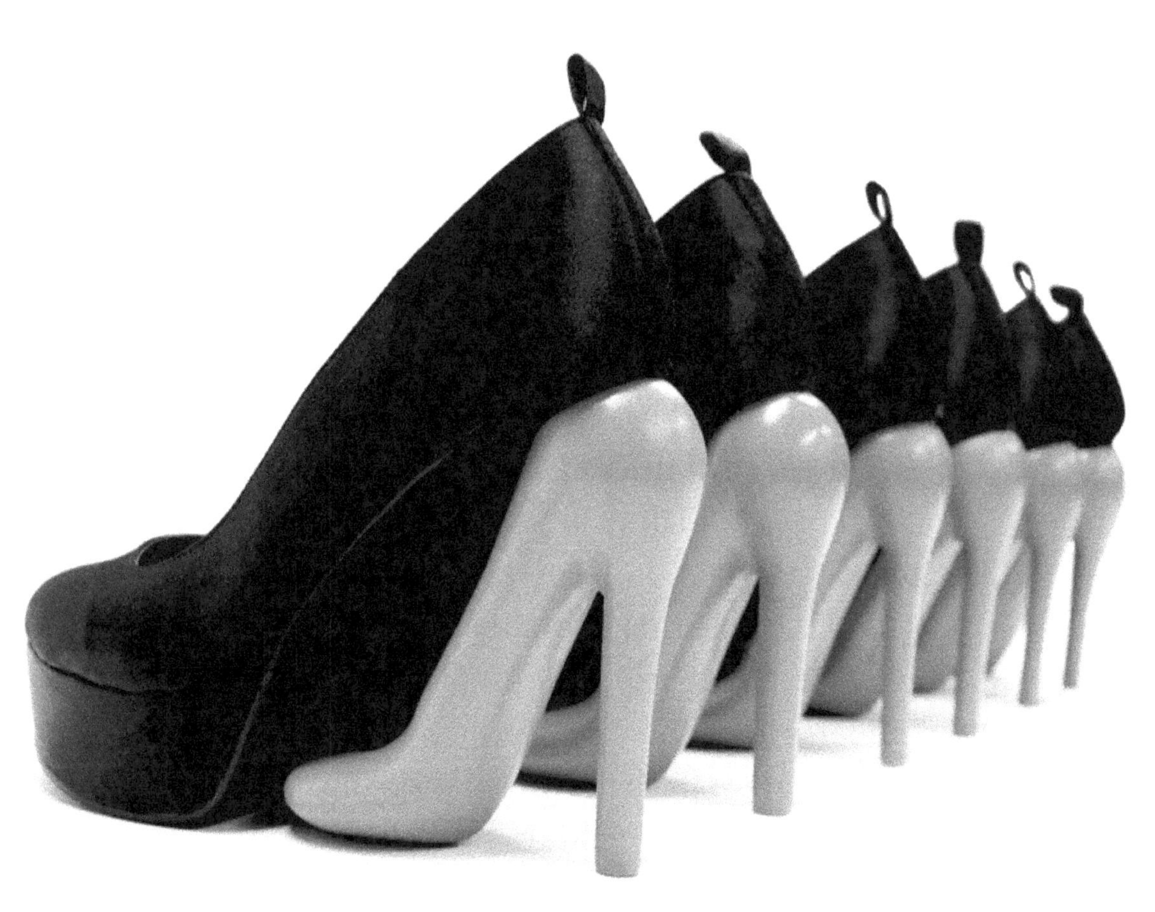

I Ain't No Poet

I ain't no poet I'm just in love
Wanting to share what oooh you share and we share...
Fire burning deep in my soul keeping the very place where you reside cozy and inviting
Anticipating each glance of your strong sensual eyes
Chasings your stare wanting to be satisfied by just one glance
I ain't no poet I'm just in love
Tingling from the afterglow of one slight mutual brush of our hands as our bodies
Crave deeper contact
I ain't no poet I'm just in love
Suspended in air
Supported by
Devotion
Desire
LOVE
I ain't no Poet I am LOVE!

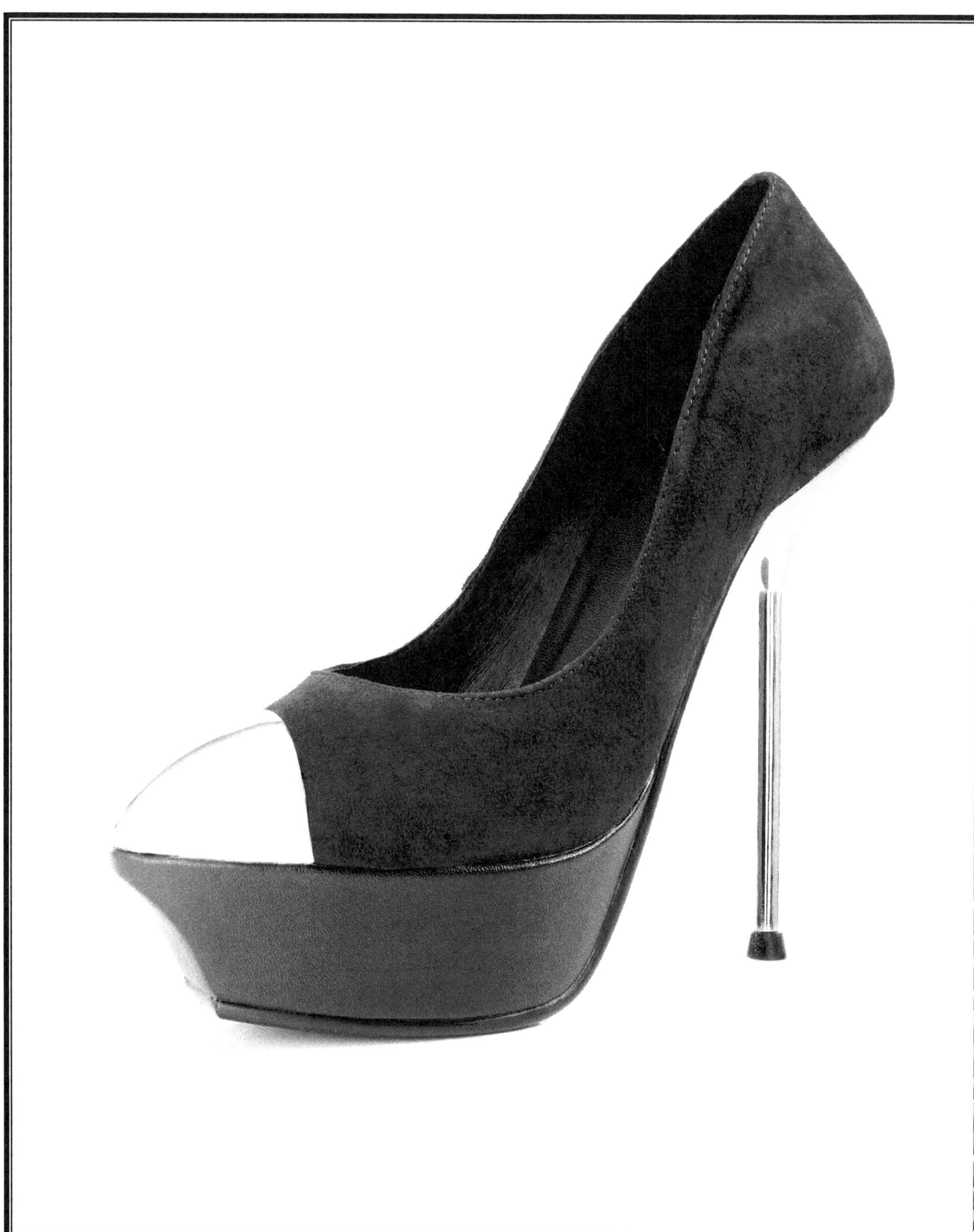

Subtle Inspiration

I sit here visualizing you in your fullness
I ponder the connection between us

You inspire me!
Making me want more of what I didn't even know
I needed

The images of your half shaded face
Delivers warm sensations piercing
My being

Your pen, a precise artistic tool
Offering up millions of sacrificial pixels
Bringing beautiful words in existence
Words that reach across thousands of miles that
Separate us
Bringing us close enough to taste each other's
Core!

So, I say to you my dear INSPIRATION
I too yearn for what you possess
Power to ignite passion in all who dare to gape at
Your abilities
Blessed by your presence

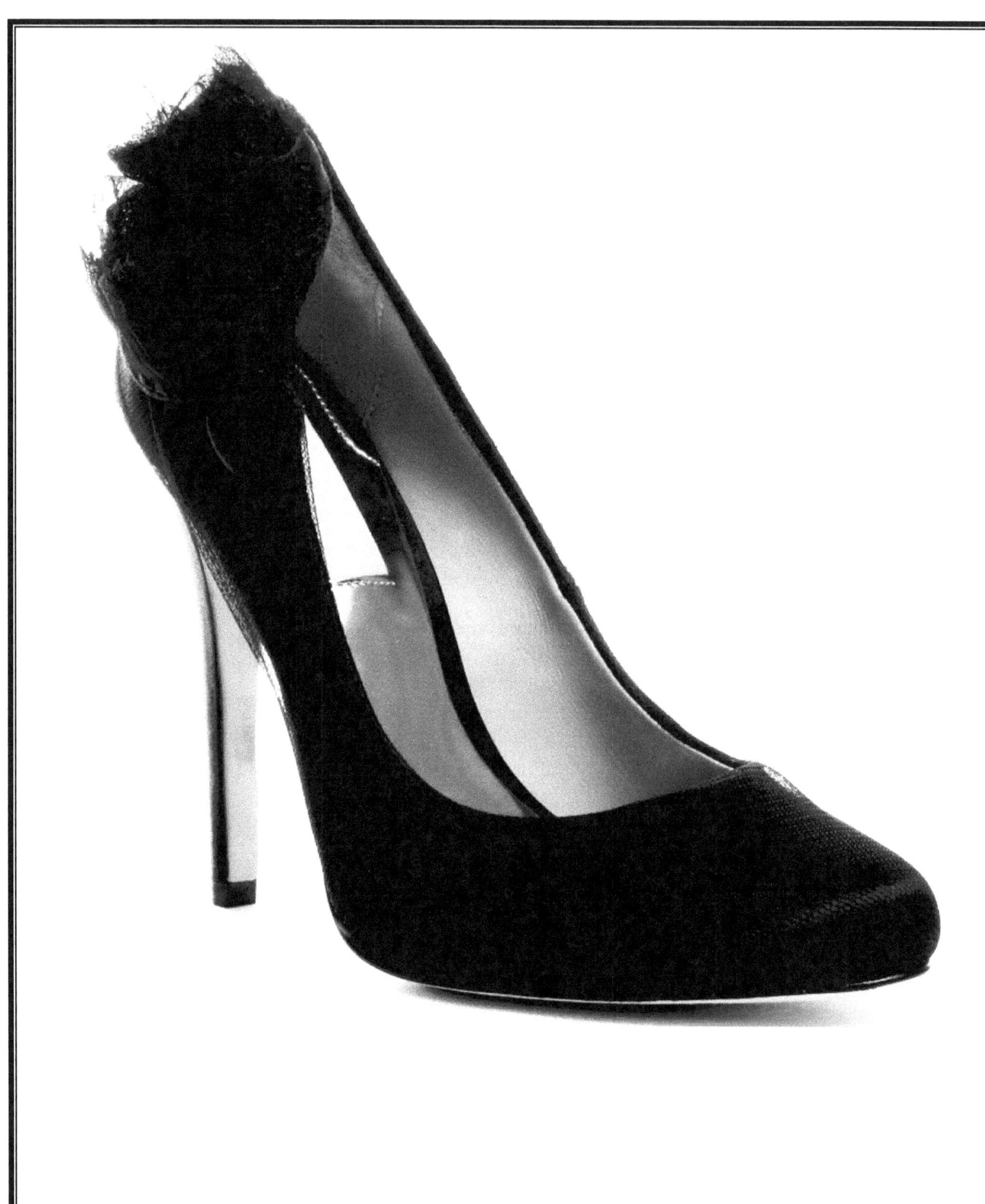

Tranquility

Soft deep relaxation
Waves of Zen
Flowing ever so gently
Cool crisp breeze
On a humid Summer's eve
Wide open arms
With a bosom of peace
Take refuge in the presence of
Tranquility

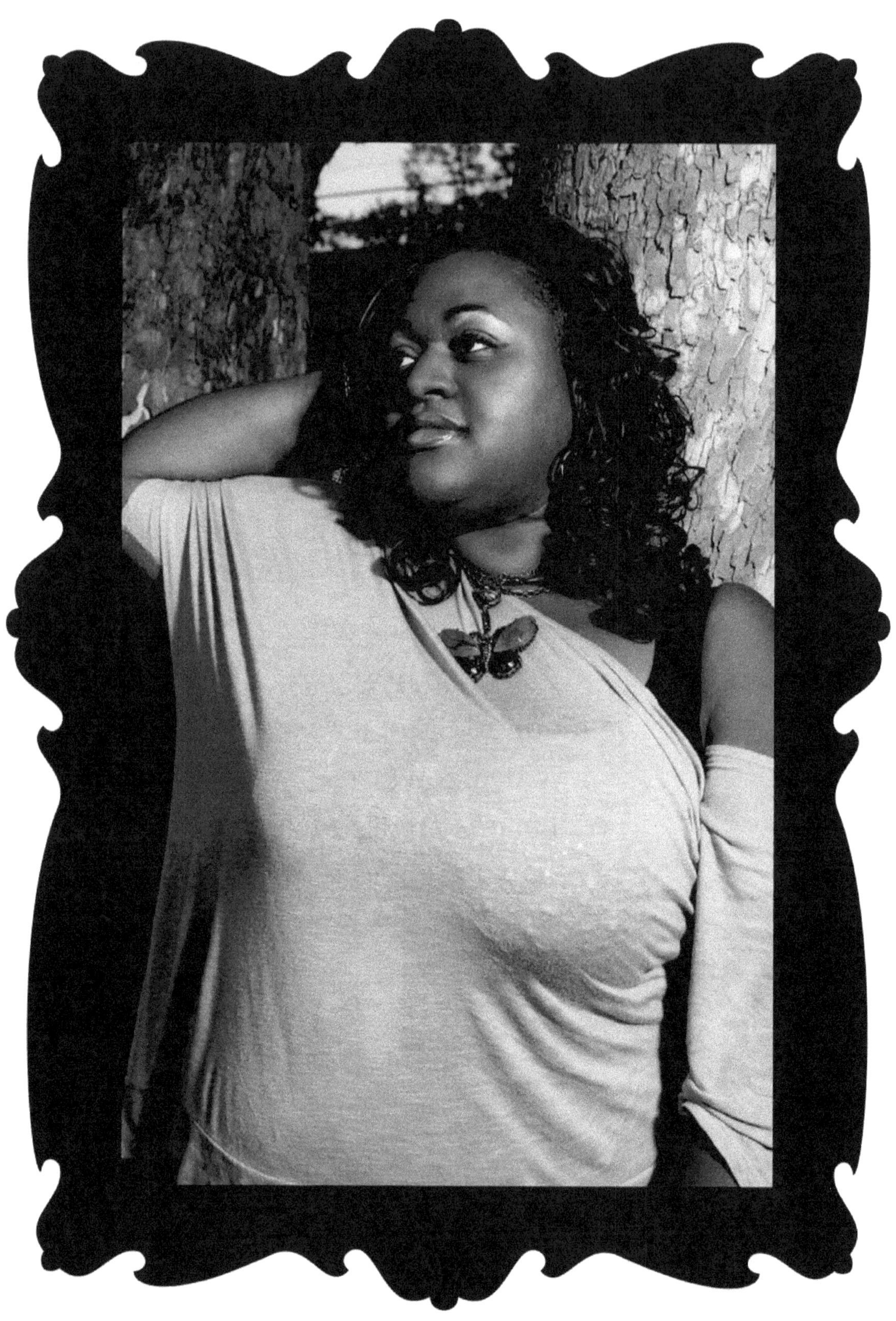

AWAKEN

I can't do this anymore... I don't feel the same
Yet I continue to surrender
My mind
My body
To dull the pain
Promises escape your full lips
Manipulative Verbiage
Urging my trust
I can't do this anymore ...
I give into you
My spirit broken as I transition into You
The image you wish for me has my being under siege
I no longer exist
Trapped in the lies of yesterday and hope for Tomorrow
I can't do this anymore...
Your love is like pretty poison
Killing me softly
Infused with conditions and no recognition
Yet my love for you is sober
I surrender all that I am
You provide a mirage of a warm embrace
As you ensure me that I complete your cycle
Convincing speech dangle from your tongue
As you urge me that you need me in your space
I search for a glimpse of myself to provide
Strength
Substance
Courage
I can't do this anymore...I don't feel the same
I caught my reflection in the mirror and it called me By another name
AWAKENED

Kia Rogers

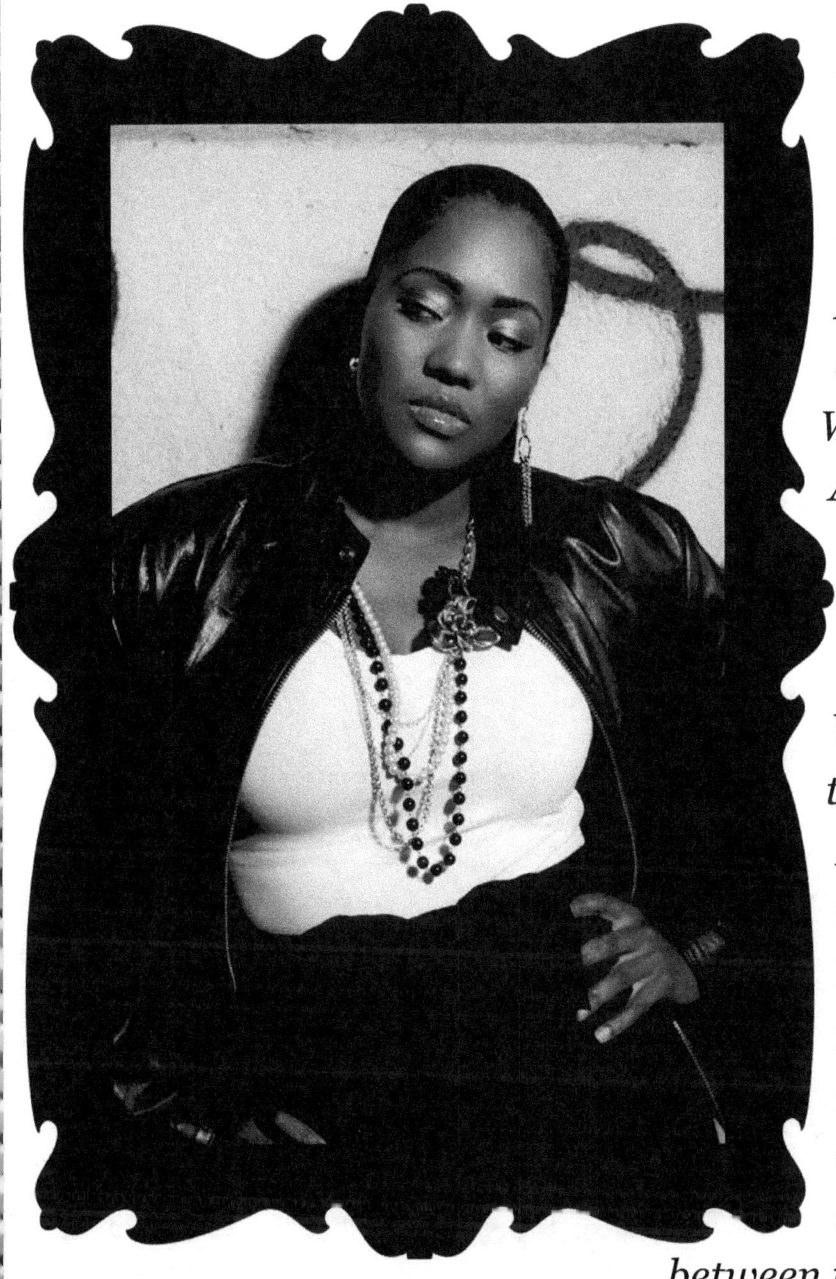

Long before I boarded my first flight, I was able to travel beyond my immediate surroundings. A pen and pad...my mode of transportation; Writing was my passport. As long as I can remember I've always been observant yet selectively outspoken. Writing has allowed me to express myself in what I would later recognize as my bold voice. Throughout my life in many if not all of my experiences, my emotional composition has always found solace between the pages of a composition book. It is with great pleasure that I share with you a glimpse of my growth, grief, and gratitude as I journey through life's trials and triumphs.

♥Kia

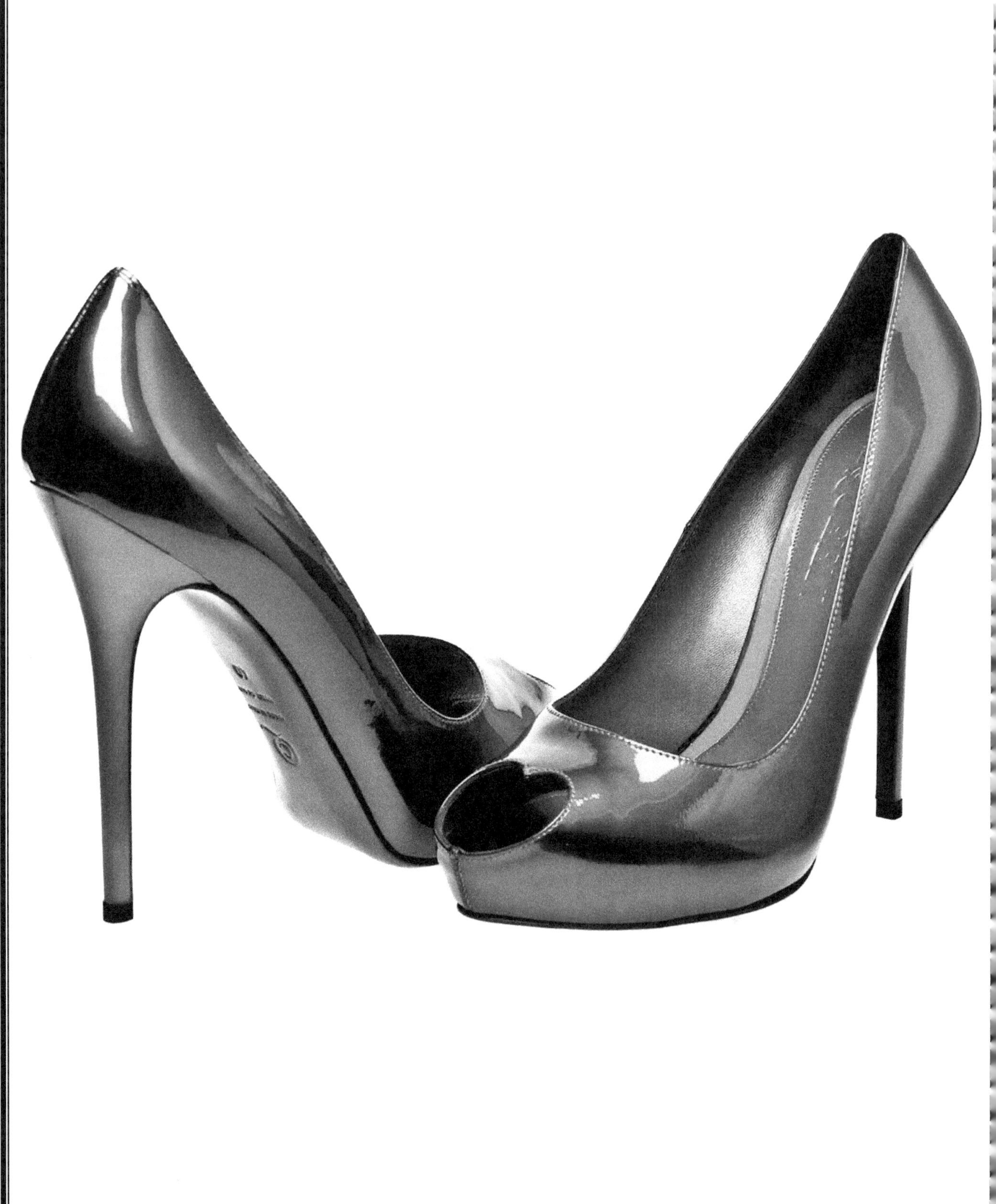

She and I

Last night **SHE** passed out inebriated in life's pain, reeking of stale perfume.
Gold dipped chains adorned her neck, green from the change of her body temperature
Soiled sheets draped her body
A pillow worn from countless nights of crying cradled her head
Her makeup atrociously covered the mattress, as if to insinuate the removal of plastered pain
The beginning of the end
Last night **SHE** became **I** and **I** became whole

Her mahogany brown skin would no longer appear bruised or sallow
For last night **SHE** dreamed in color for the first time and discovered living and being alive are two separate entities
Last night **SHE** passed out feeling like
The salt of mankind wounds
This morning **I** awoke feeling like the salt of the earth!

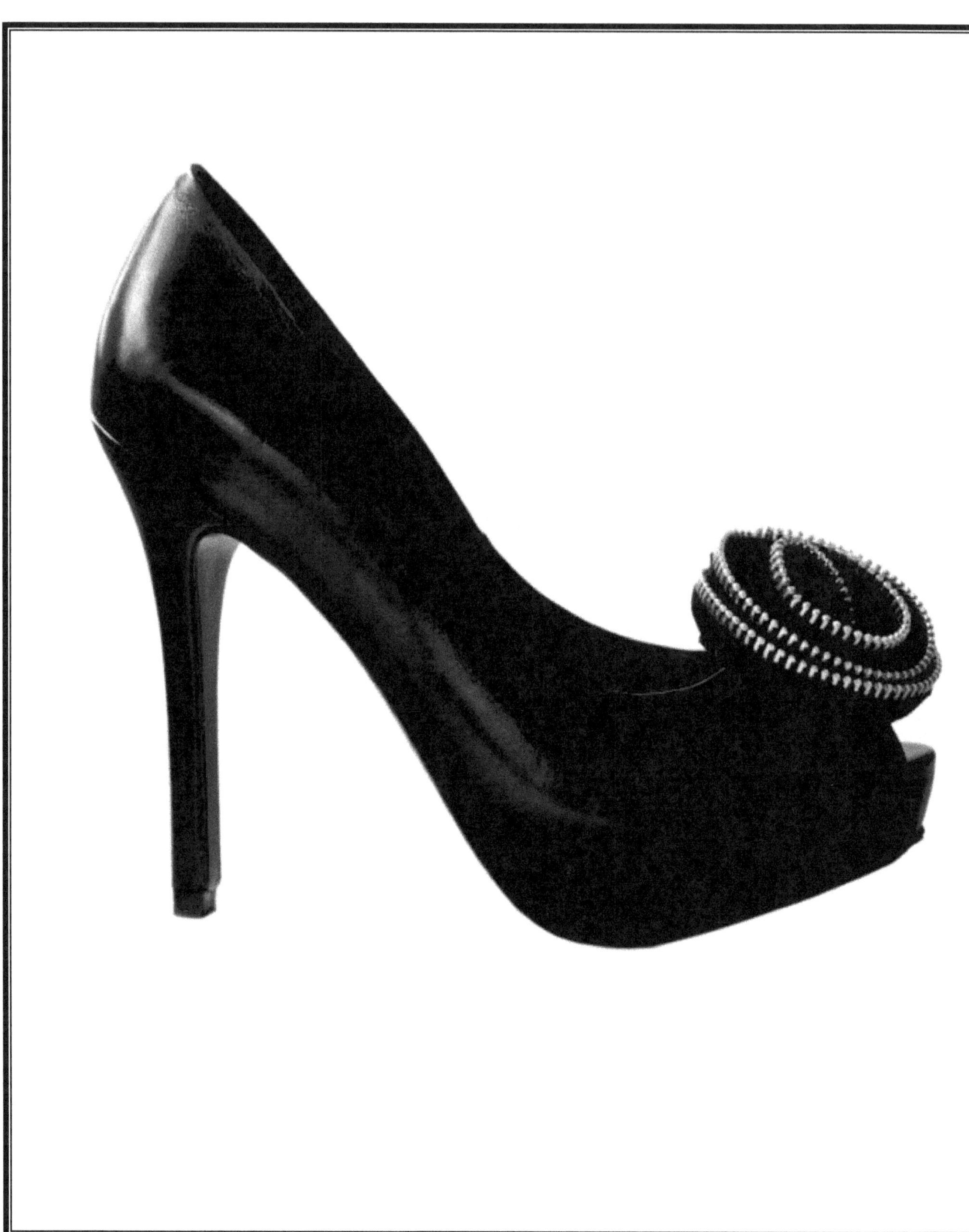

NO JUDGMENT…JUST OBSERVATION

The reality is, were living in a Technicolor nightmare
Still chasing the original American dream
The Dream has been remixed

Neighborhoods have become battlefields
Playgrounds...land mines
Schools... Boot camps & Breeding grounds

We're fighting a war we didn't sign up for
We were drafted by birth

No Judgment, Just Observations

There is a platform for you to be heard
A platform for leadership...We have the right to vote
Education is paramount! Our Public school system is deteriorating
Each passing day
There is a lottery going on, without tickets
There is 2,000 applicants 42 spots
Will you read between the lines or count how many future statistics that leaves behind

No Judgment, Just Observations

We've developed a false sense of purchasing power
Living out black card fantasies, in reality were existing at the bottom in the red...Nice shoes by the way!

No Judgment, Just Observations

Mothers and Fathers have traded in nurturing for neglect
Virtues and values for material trappings
Lovers and friends have become tricks and johns
Women have forgotten how to be ladies
Men have forgotten what it means to be a Man
Cover your women and children

No Judgment, Just Observations

We're making a mockery of our beliefs
Pretending to love while pursuing Lust
Raising Hell on Saturday
Begging for Heaven on Sunday
Garbed up...stripped down
Protesting, don't worry about how I raise my children, when I went to church or if I made Salah...don't judge me!
We judge one another with our whispers and stares on everything from our hair to our wears

No Judgment, Just Observation.

I refuse to apologize to for my opinion
Perhaps you sensed my frustration in how I projected
My intention wasn't to offend, I just Pray you were affected

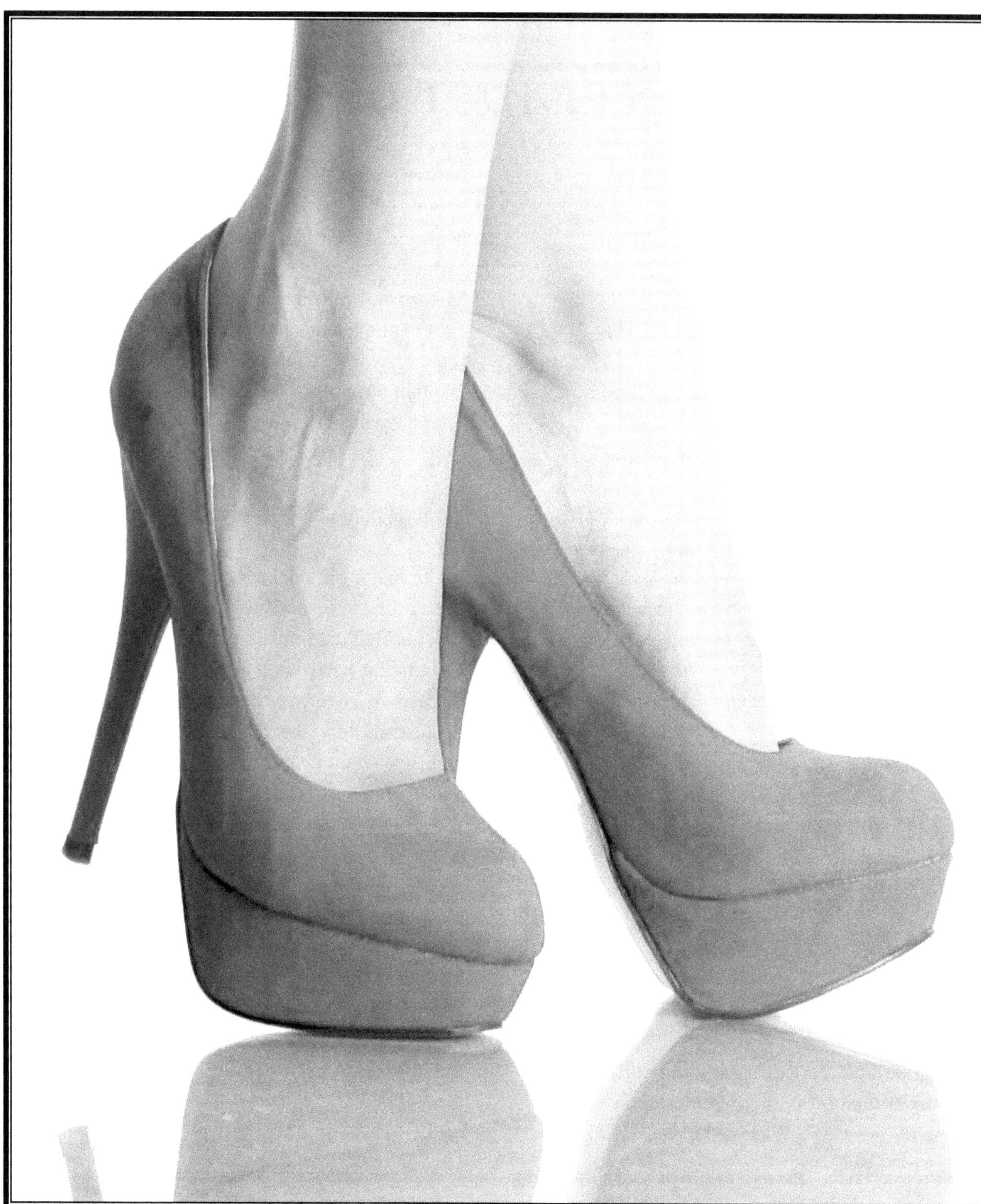

X to Y Chromosome!

How would you feel? If...
I caressed your body with imagery
Massaged your soul with support
Captivated your mind with my essence
Tickled your fancy with a smile
Made you scream silently through tears
Moan abruptly through sweat; or
Hypnotized you with delicate movements of my
Silhouette

Would this be LOVE? Or just good SEX

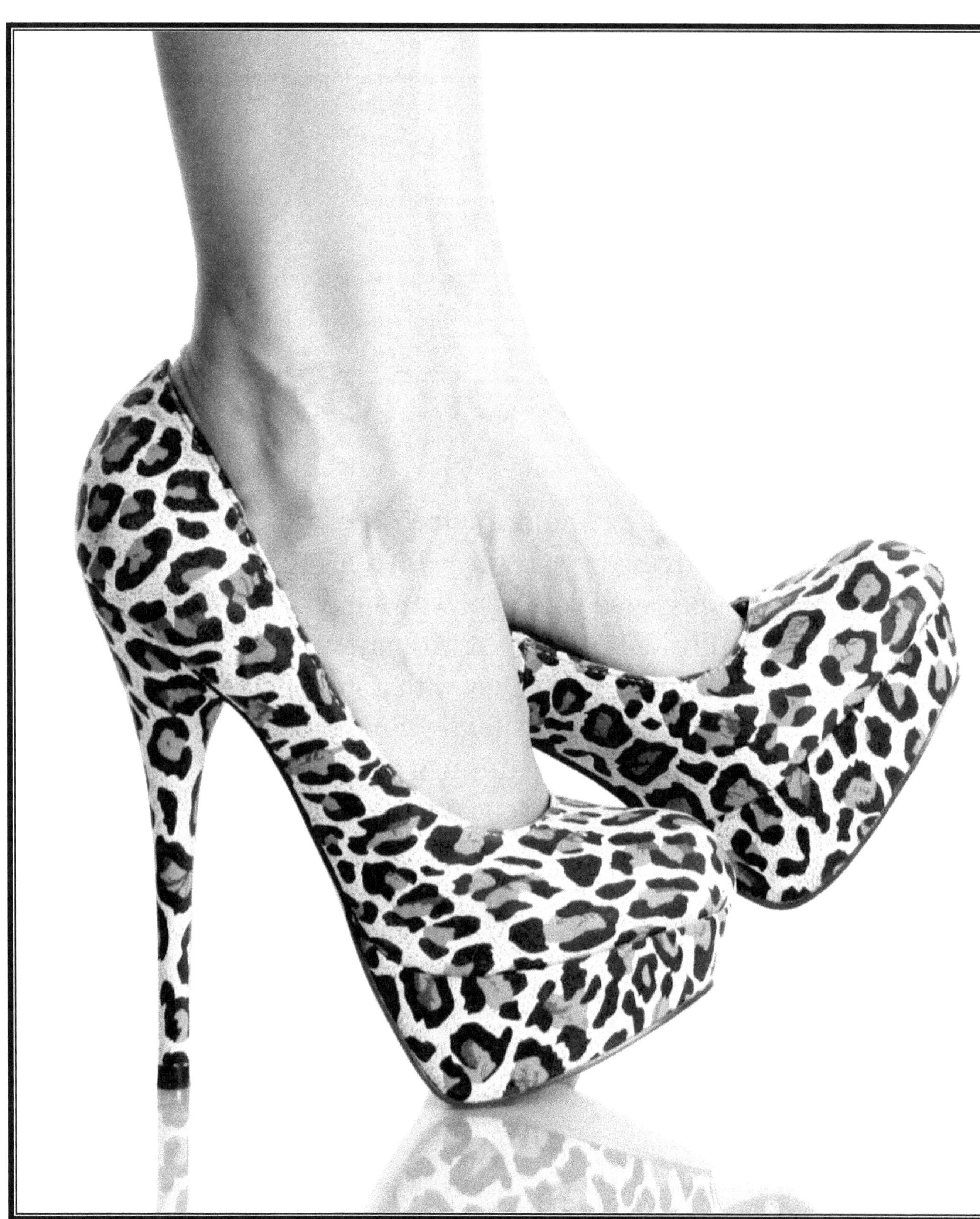

Just Wondering

I often wonder what it would be like to truly be free
Free from the seclusion of my thoughts of you

I often wonder what provokes the anxiety I feel at just the mental sight of you
I see no physical characteristics yet I feel you embracing me heart first

I often reflect on countless conversations I've had with you in silence over stolen glances

I often reminisce on times when I've become so aroused with intrigue you stifle my impatience only to influence my desire to be with you beyond capacity

I often wonder how at times when I've felt emotionally naked you'd suddenly appear before me & clothe me in admiration and assurance

I've often wondered when I'm lost in life's crowd how you'd somehow manage to filter your way inside me
Rescue me from obscurity and wisp me away to tranquility

I often wonder why at the slightest hint of rain no matter where I'm standing I immediately imagine each drop pattering against the windowpane as I eagerly anticipate your arrival

I often envision myself neatly draped all over you like imported silk fit for royalty

I often wonder how is it that I've never actually felt your hands yet you've somehow touched me in ways that I've never fathomed

I was just wondering

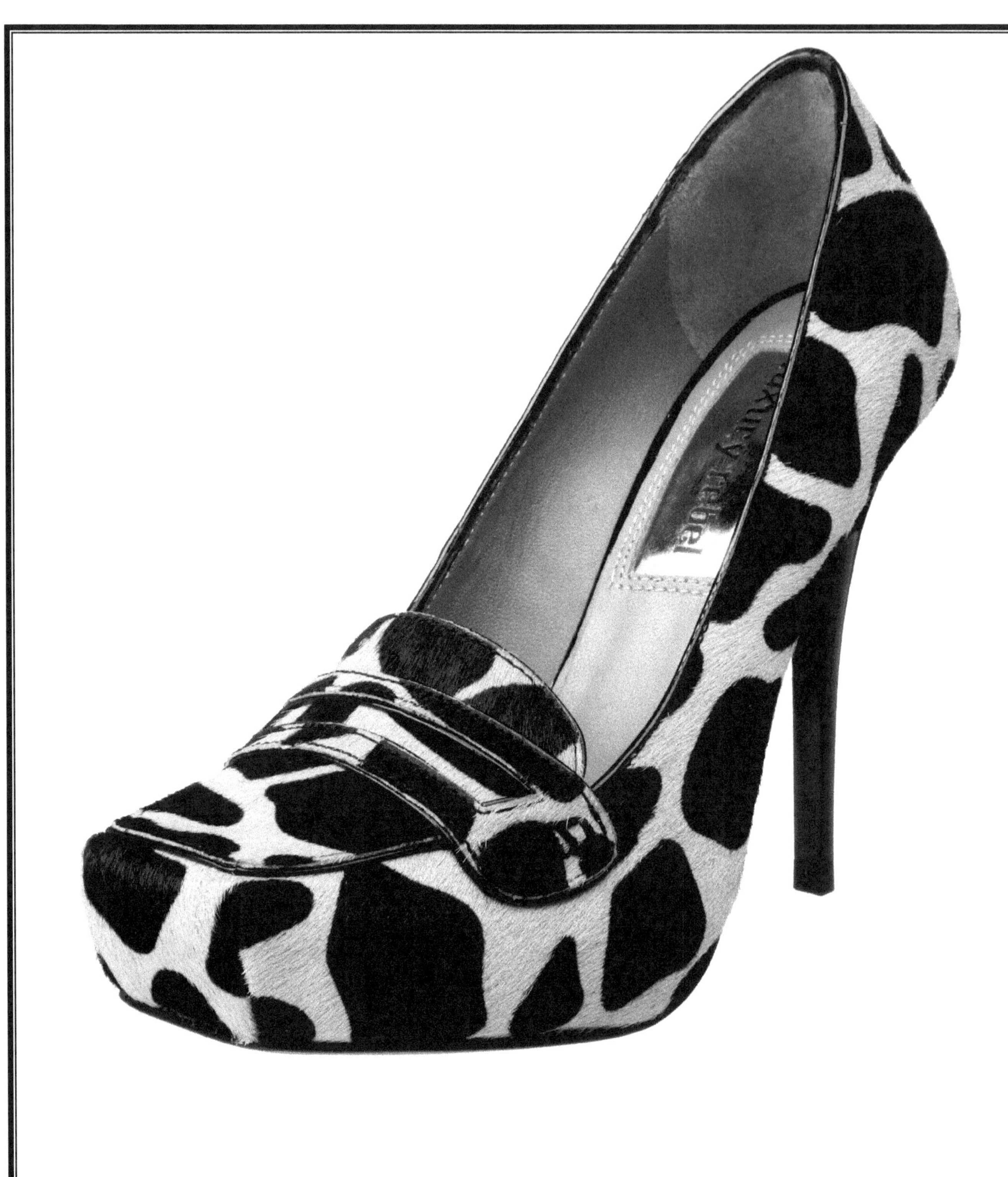

The Rapture

Your Love is a familiar face in a crowded room
Warm with conversation
Enchanting as wild orchids in full bloom

It is slow motion at fast pace
It is timeless ecstasy in open space

It is extraordinary as rainbows after hard rain
It is a beam of sunshine
Comfort for heartache and pain

It is the gentle innocence of your touch
Priceless as penny candy
Special like my first crush

It is the strength of black coffee
No sugar, no cream
It is a deep sleep with an uninterrupted dream

It is the beauty of sunset
The blessing of sunrise
It is the splendor of nature
The power of a rising tide

It is the abundance of the rapture
The thrill of the chase
The excitement of the capture

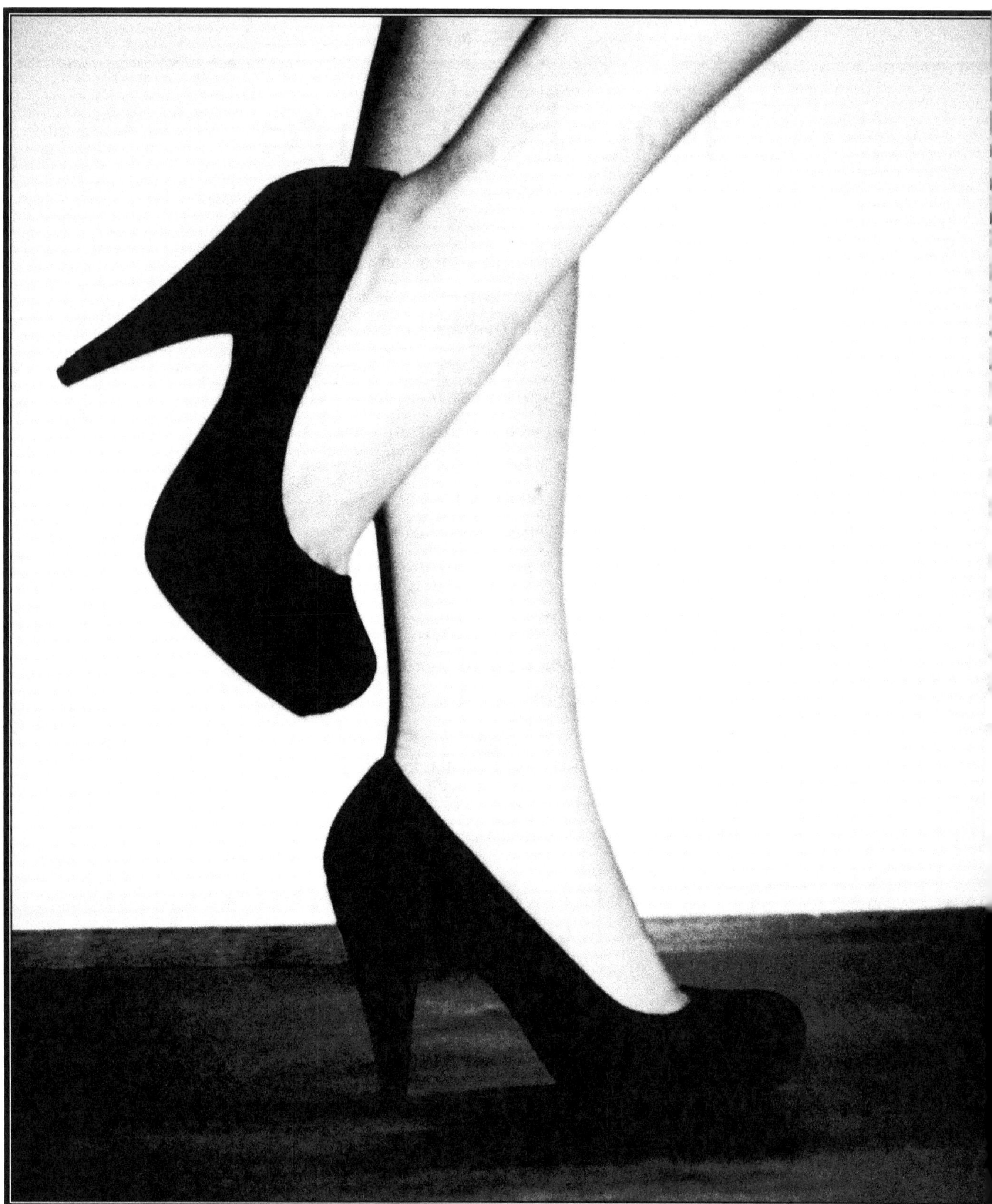

Wrath of the Rainbow

I got caught up in the wrath of the rainbow.
Distracted by his deep rich BROWN skin
Intoxicated with his RED passion kiss
Mesmerized by the heat of his ORANGE warm touch
Infatuated with his GREEN generosity
Hypnotized by his YELLOW promises...our future seemed so bright

My PURPLE heart beat loyal to him
My only truth his WHITE lies over sips of liquid GOLD
Allowed my PINK rosebud to bloom for him
Discovering its merely a Black hole to him
There is no light at the end of that tunnel, no pot of GOLD rings that is at the bottom of that rainbow

Only my shadow in hues of BLUE
I got caught up in the wrath of the rainbow
Don't let it happen to you!

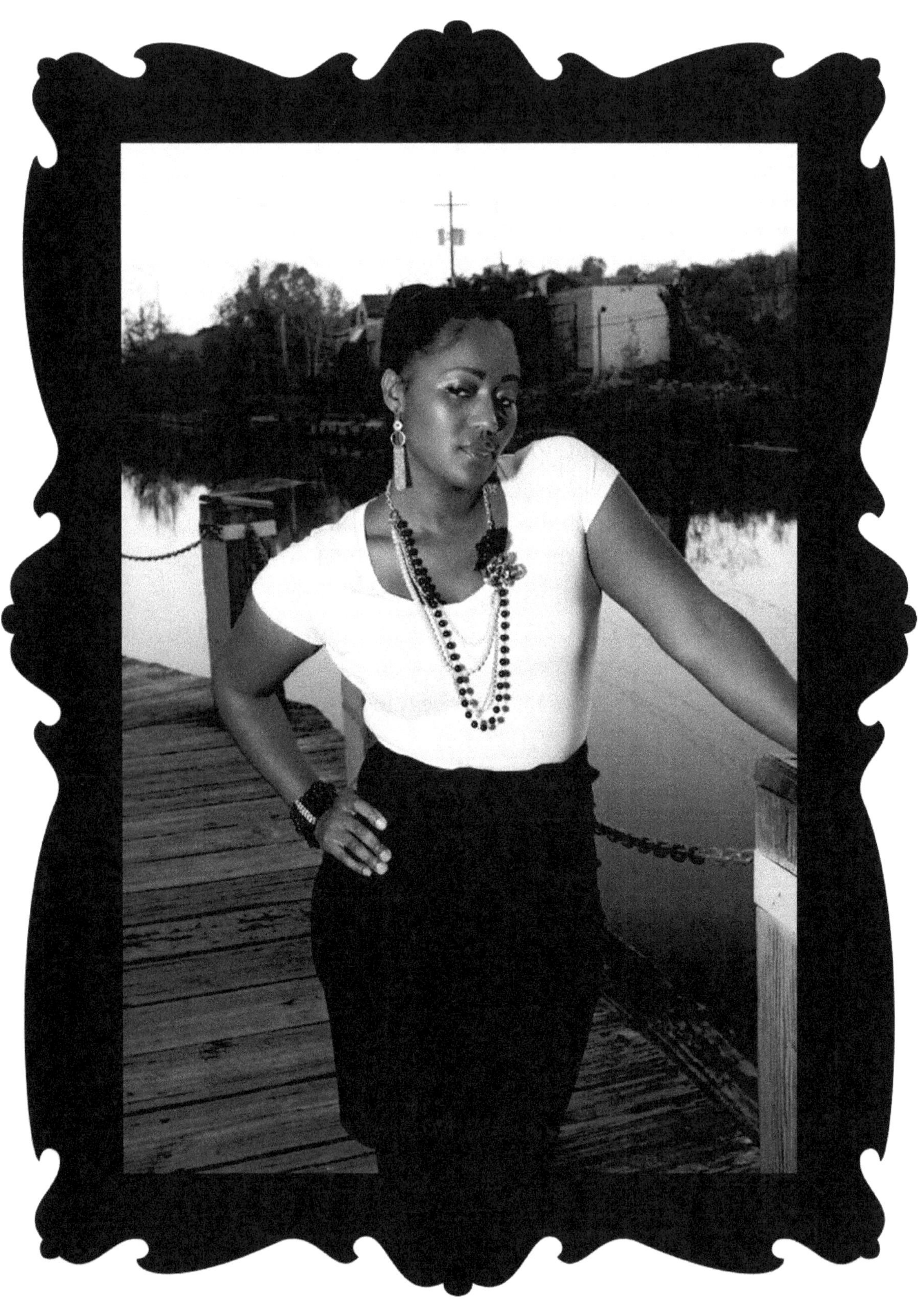

A Self Discovery: The Woman You're Supposed to Be

When you dream, you dream in black and white, you doubt yourself forsaking the colors of your ability, allowing bleakness to become your light

When you cry, you cry in silence relieving yourself on the inside, you dismiss your feelings and disregard your tears as a dishonor to your pride

When you encounter distress you beguile yourself with gage and under extreme circumstances, you respond with uncertainty and react on impulse in rage

When you look in the mirror you don't see effortless beauty, nor endless possibilities, you see yourself as inadequate and make note of your inabilities

When you embark on things that are wonderful, you stifle and become so unsure, you sneer in disbelief and convince yourself of reasons why these things are not to be endured

When you examine yourself, you overlook the potential you, leaving yourself to remain unseen, for you do not wish to see, you ignore yourself in shame...in fear of becoming the woman your supposed to be

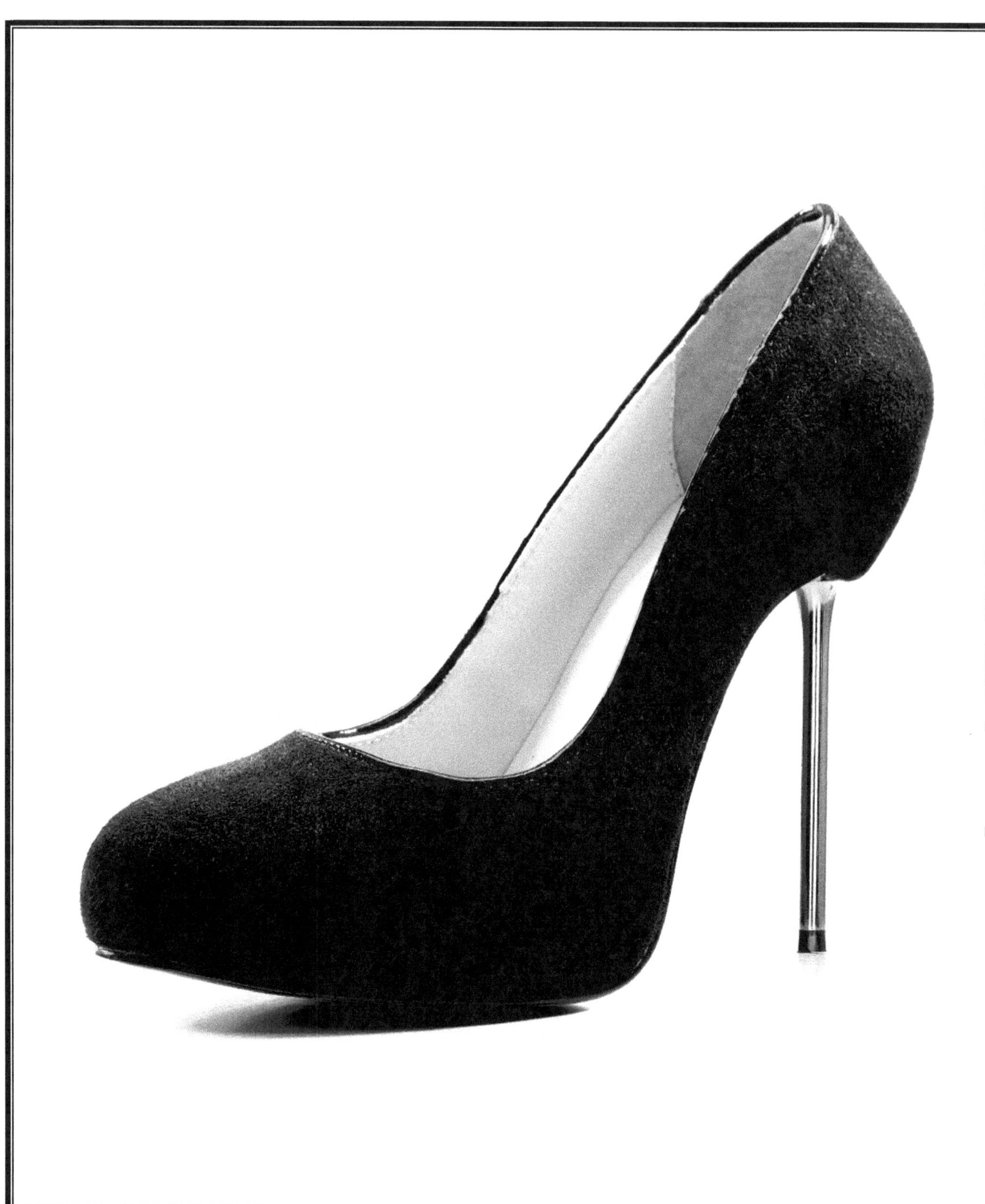

Breakfast in Bed

This morning I gave my man breakfast in bed; I became his morning paper ready to be opened and read at 6:00am

He read me from the headlines to the sports page skipping the classifieds...there was no help wanted

Until this morning coffee was his only addiction... then I gave him something else strong and black

He usually grabs donuts on the go; I gave him a reason to stay and my own sweet sticky something with a creamy center

He thought he liked his eggs scrambled and fluffy; until I showed him why they taste better sunny side up

He told me he craved French toast with brown sugar and fruit from time to time

I told him I'm always browned to perfection and even better with syrup
As for fruit it's not the only thing ripe & healthy

Finally he told me he had to have his fresh squeezed orange juice.
I told him orange juice isn't the only thing that provides vitamin C...
When breakfast was finished he knew that I offered balance & he should never start his day without me

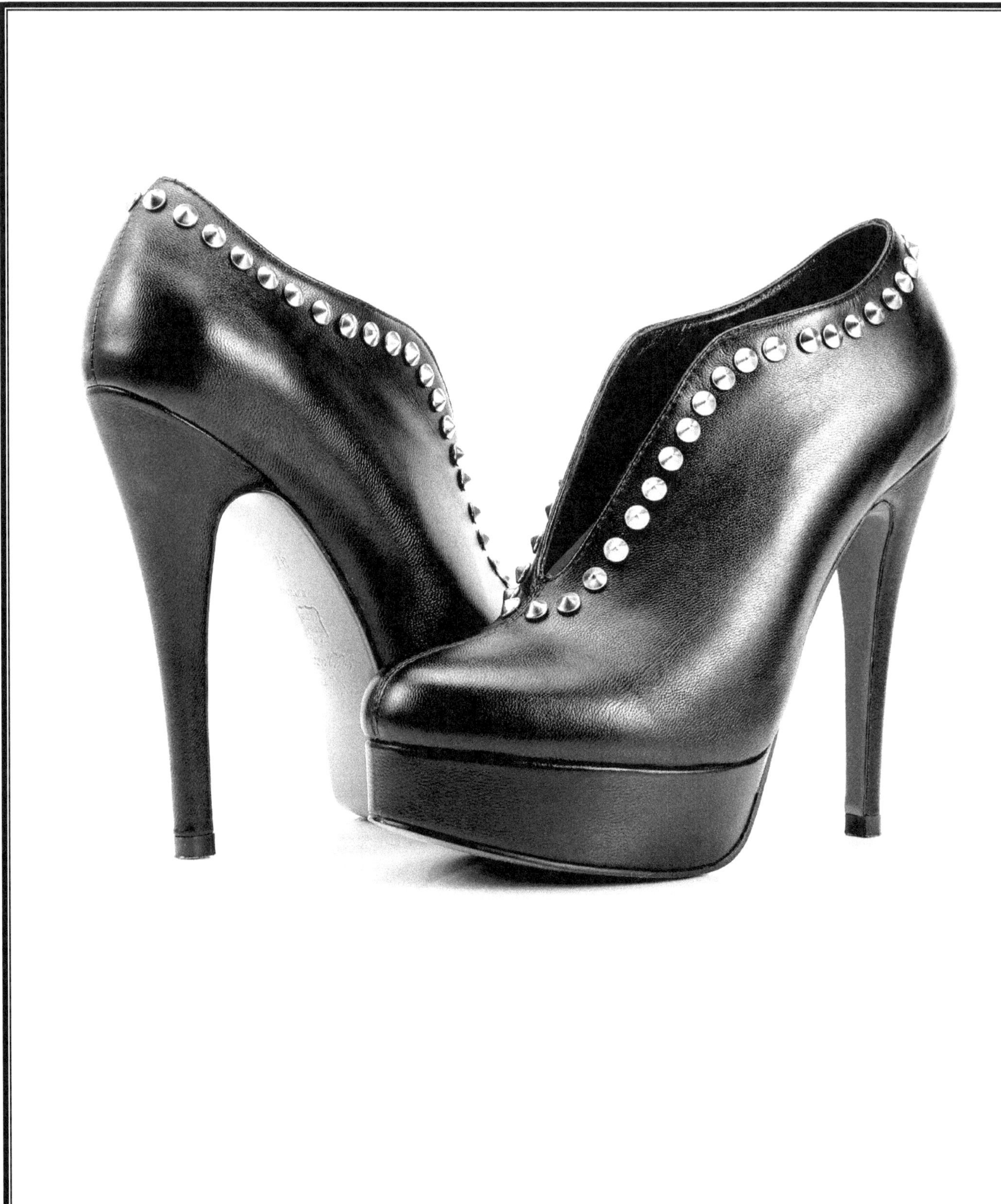

Closure

I dialed his number and hung up...
I dialed his number knowing he had caller ID and hung up

The method...for him to see my name and acknowledge my presence
The madness... for him to see my name and acknowledge my absence

I **wanted** him to feel the same distance I've felt
I **wanted** him to wonder why I didn't follow up with conversation
I **wanted** him to be distracted from whatever or whomever he was doing
I **wanted** him to recognize the part my of his actions that warranted my reaction
I **wanted** him to get a sense of how it feels to be confused and uncertain
I **wanted** him to dial my number and reopen the lines of communication
I **wanted** him to feel me reaching out to him on his level
I **wanted** him to take stock of himself, just as I had of myself

I **needed** to stop reveling in his mind games
I **needed** to stop endorsing his excuses for his shortcomings
I **needed** to tell him how deeply I love him with conviction
I **needed** to tell him if he and I were no longer us, I'd be hurt, I'd even cry, and yet I'd be alright
I **needed** to stop wanting so much of what he is unable or unwilling to share. I needed to move on

I WANTED CLOSURE

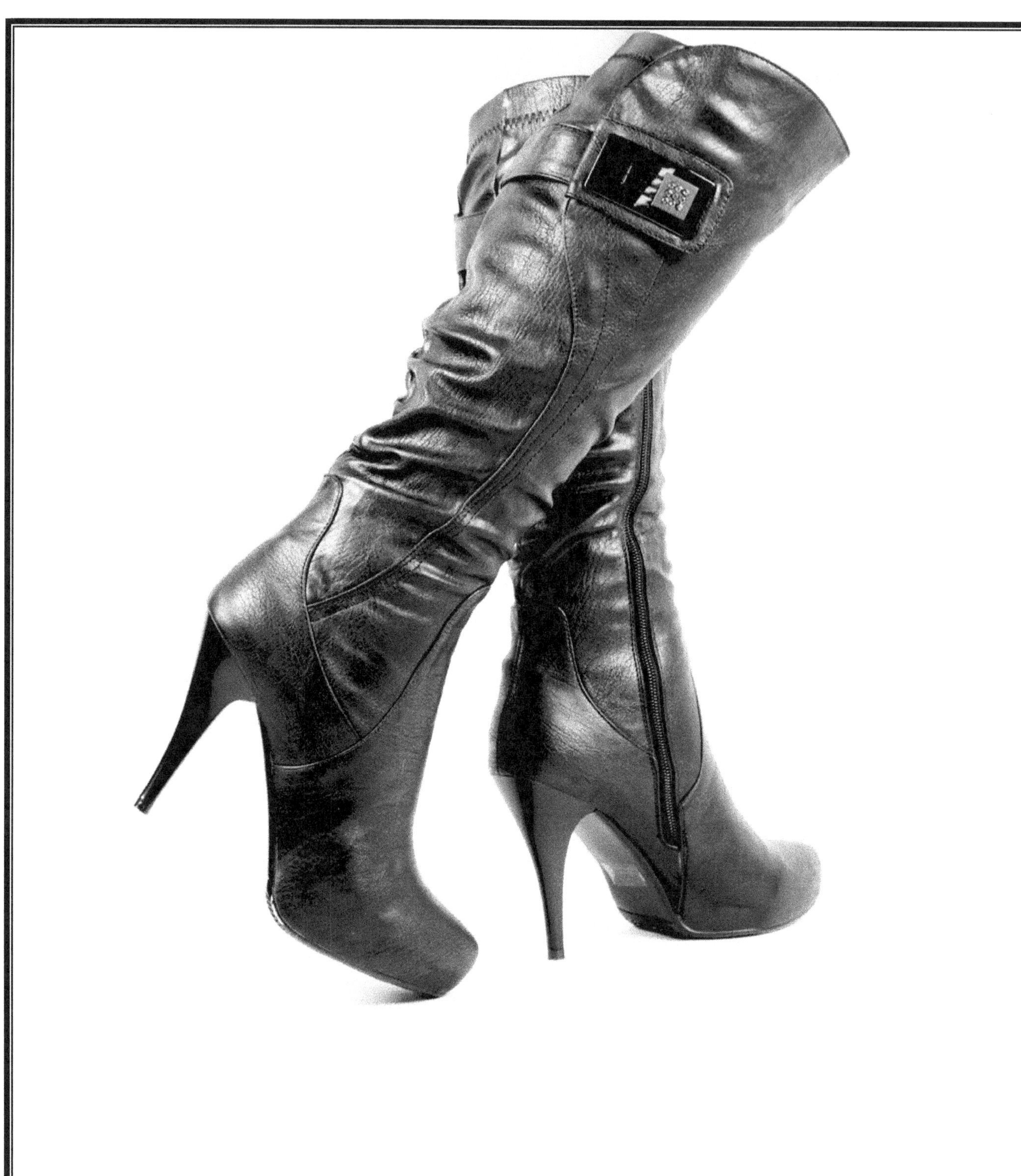

Dear Lover

If eyes are the window to the Soul, Tears must be the cleansing of the Spirit
Last night I had an internal cleansing in addition to giving birth
Rebirth of self
Only this time I did not come into the world
I came into my own
Upon my arrival I discovered the cancer of my emotional well-being
The cancer was a combination of the choices
I've made in relation to you
The result of your presence in my life

Your love has been an addiction to me
A habit of dependency of your approval, attention and affection
That is until now
I am stronger
For all the times you ignored me when I've initiated communication
Trying to tell you what I
Required, needed, wanted, felt and desired
I am stronger

For all the nights I've submerged myself in troubled water
Attempting to soak away the pain of insecurity within our relationship
I am stronger

For all the nights I've drank until the point of inebriation to become sober of my love for you
I am stronger
In closing I somehow feel compelled to thank you
For your part in my emotional evolution
I share with you the breakdown of a woman

When a woman feels anything less than priority to the man in her life
It creates a void
Where there is a void
There is emptiness
Where there emptiness
There is space
Where there is space
There is vacancy
Where there is vacancy
There is availability
Where there is availability
There is vulnerability
Where there is vulnerability
There is opportunity
Where this opportunity
Someone is wanting and waiting to explore the possibilities

P.S Never underestimate the strength of a woman

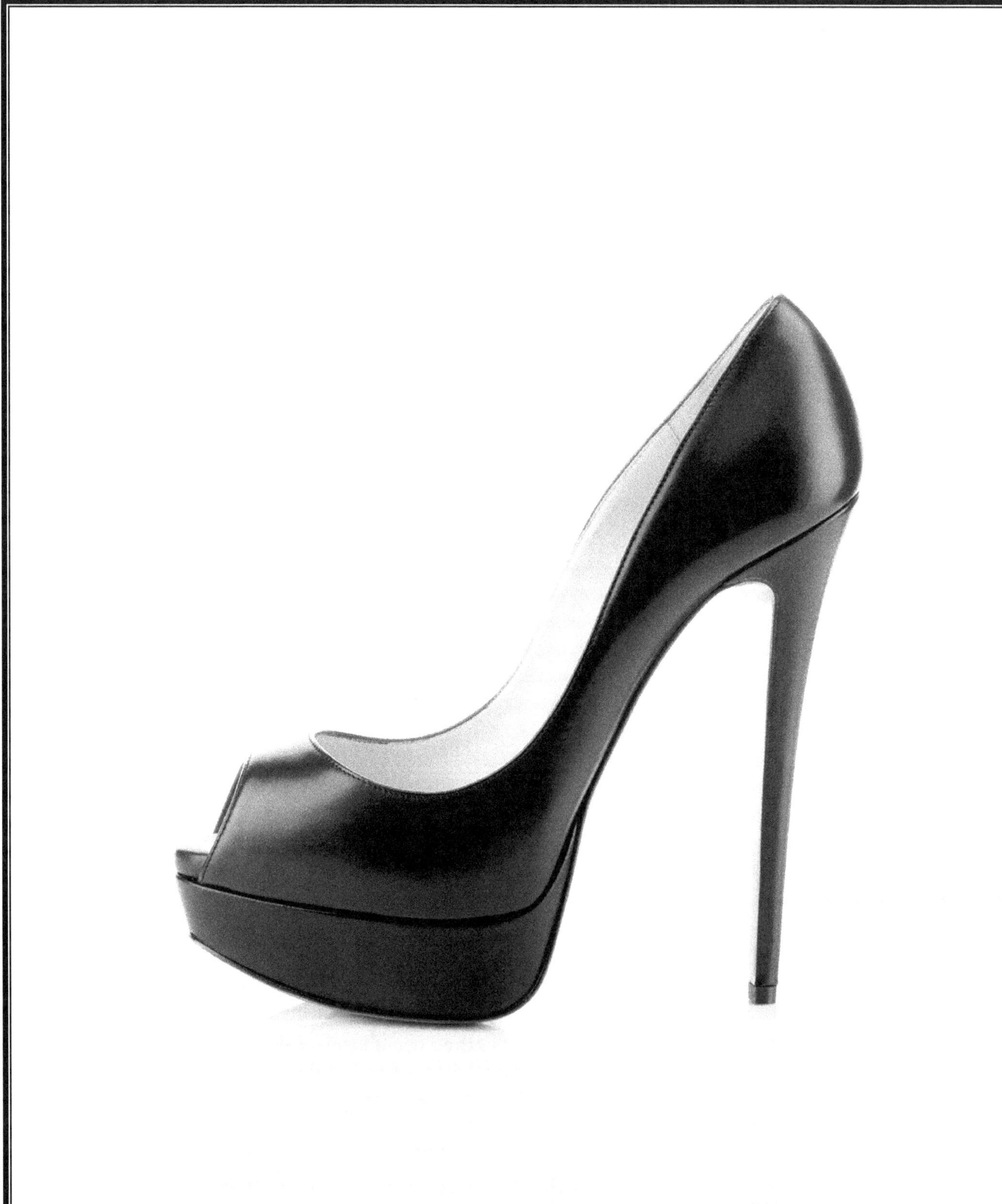

False Security

He has a graceful presence that warrants no introduction
A strong silent man
He carries a silence so profound you want to listen and projects a voice so soothing its borders manipulation

His loving is brisk and piercing as a winter day
As fresh and new as a spring breeze,
As sweet and sticky as a summer evening
As comforting as cashmere on fall afternoon
As necessary as the air we breathe
He finds beauty in my imperfections and tells me he loves me in tones of such urgency
Each breath I take becomes a labor of love

He loves me in a manner that surpasses sweeping me off of my feet
It is a degree of allure that could steal your heart away
Elegantly draped in charm so magnetic you willingly give your soul away

He shares the kind of loving that makes you want to sleep on the wet spot
For nothing more than to savor the passion from wince it was created

Each time he holds me it's as if I'm lying down to die
Time after time being more heavenly than the last

It's the kind of love one could easily get lost in
The type of circumstance that scratches the surface rarely reaching the core
It's the kind of love I sometimes enjoy in the meantime

Without any expectation of a lifetime

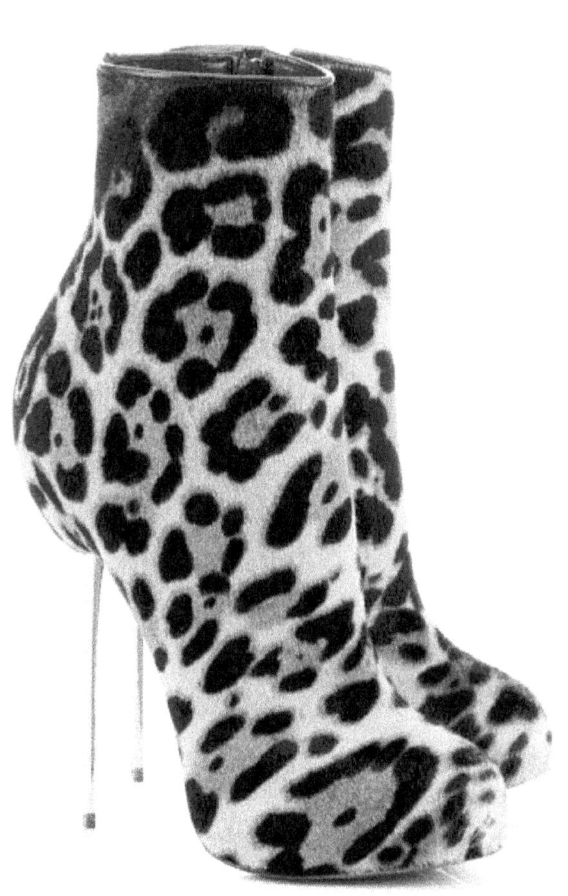

In the Best Of Company

In the best of company I am myself,
relaxed yet aware
Able to be sociable only to you find
you and I are the only people here

In the best of company there are no
blank stares just warm exchanges
however you and I are the only ones
here

In the best of company I am able to
Laugh heartily
Smile profusely
Surrender my vulnerability
Disclose my emotions forthright and
have no questions asked

In your presence I find comfort in
knowing this too shall pass

In the best of company I am able to
simper silently or weep in sorrow in
the embrace of your warmth
I am able to reflect on yesterday in
preparation of tomorrow

In the best of company I am at a
distinct peace within
I am able to recognize life's paths are
truly divine

In the best of company I am able to
acknowledge lonely as a friend of
mine

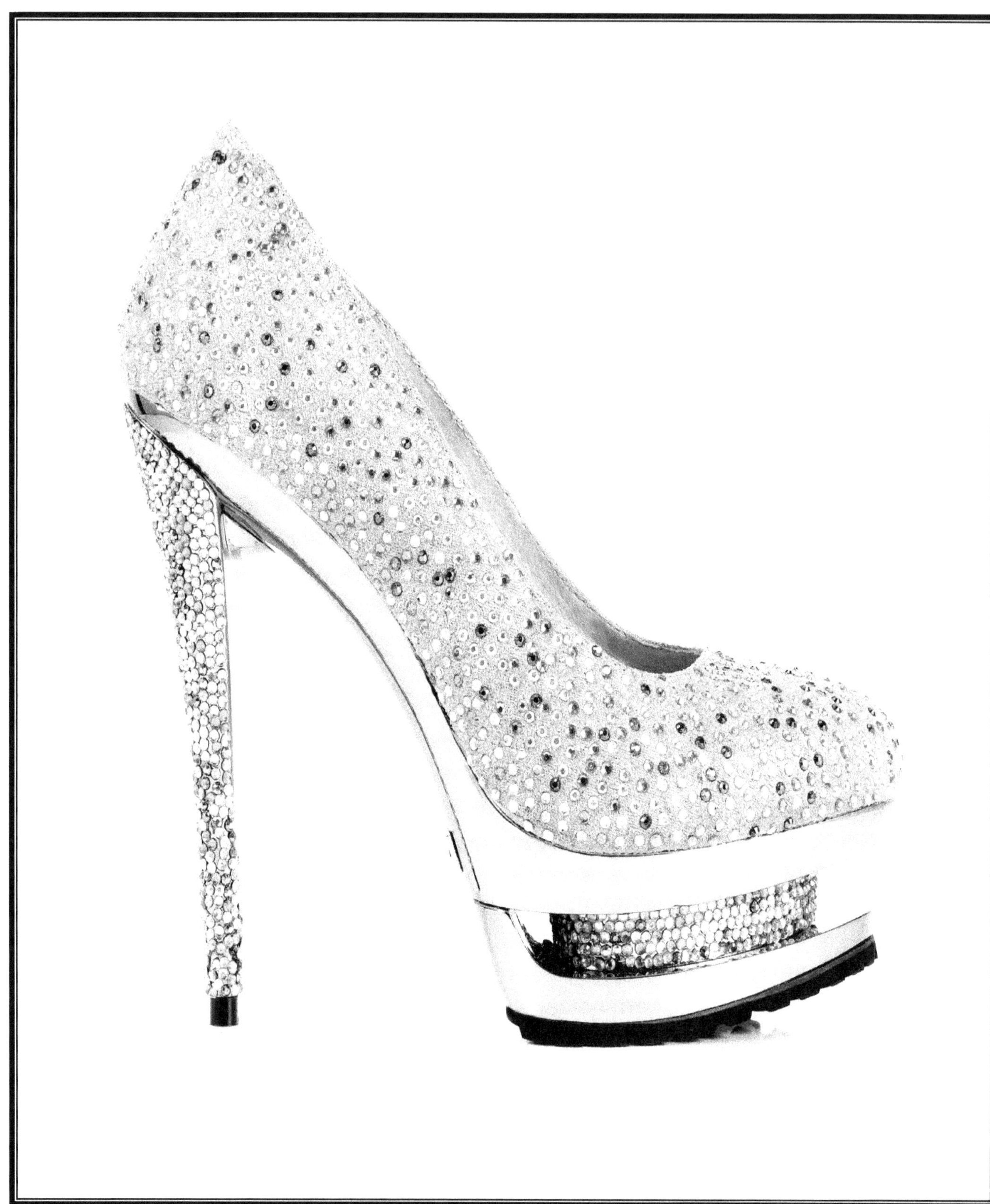

Love at its Demise

So many times I cried out to you never saying a word, for denial prevailed over reality, leaving my pain and suffering to remain unheard

For so long I looked to you for love and nurturing desiring only the fruits of your love to feed; unaware it has been you that I've fed; and you in need of me

On so many occasions I desired to be free yet fear of loneliness enslaved me

For so long I needed for this to work, therefore I accepted the emotional abuse and learned to tolerate being hurt

I had so many expectations I began living in fictional times, entrapping myself in a whirlwind of romance that existed only in the corners of my mind

LAST NIGHT I CRIED IN SILENCE

However today I said goodbye to fantasy and welcomed reality, I looked into your eyes and for the first time I truly realized our love has come to its demise

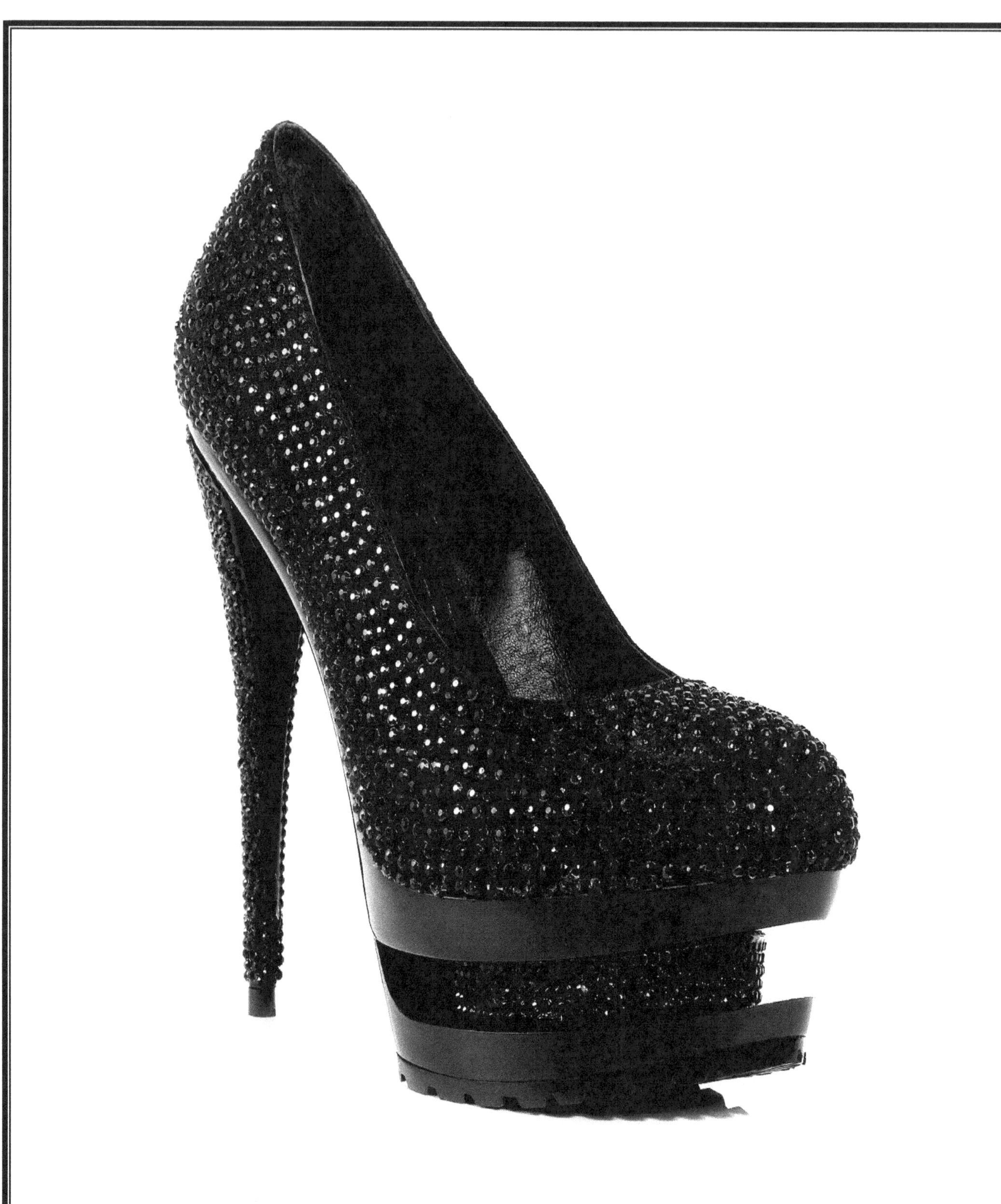

Maestro (Mystro)

He introduced himself as creative, so I told him I was Melody
He suggested we get together and harmonize sometimes
I offered my demo
He preferred live
He informed with the type of music he orchestrates timing is everything
He told me most of his masterpieces were created before the dawn of day....

We agreed to meet on the other side of midnight
That way we'd both be relaxed and more in tune with our instruments

I arrived promptly just after midnight
He applauded my coming in on the right note
I told him I needed to warm up
When I was ready I'd invite him to join me
He stood off to the side beating his drums and stroking his guitar
When he finally struck the right chord we began to play together
He played me as if I were a grand piano
Stroking each key skillfully yet delicately
He helped me reach notes I hadn't hit before

He performed with me in a manner I could never accomplish as a soloist

I entered the session as an alto with the rawness of a blues background

I exited the experience as a soprano with a classical sophistication

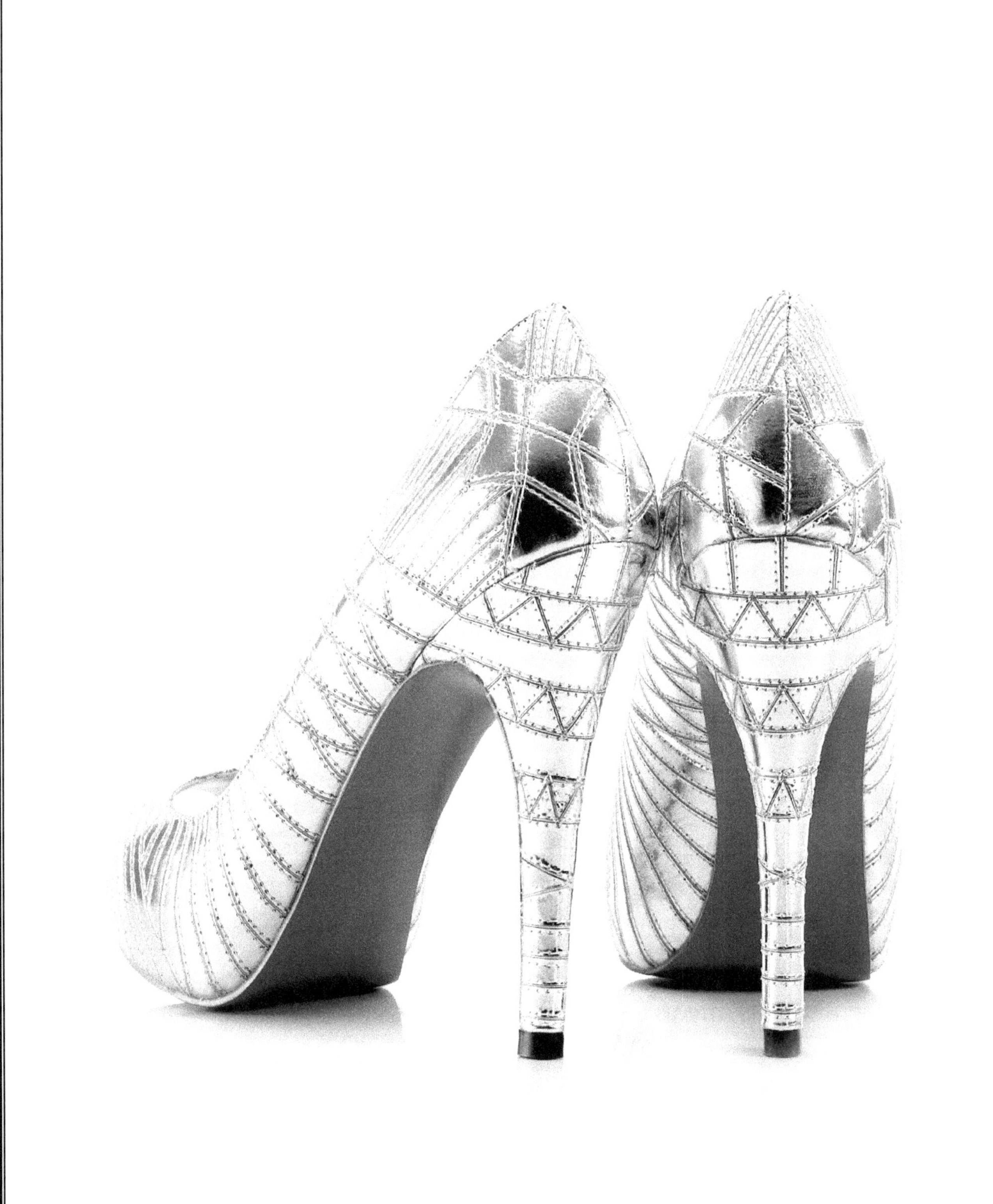

Sense

I SEE you and tell myself, what's new becomes old and what's old becomes useful again
So I'll hold onto to you like a vintage photograph waiting to be retouched

I HEAR your voice and absorb you, like a sponge absorbing cold water on a hot surface

I SMELL your natural body scent, and pack you inside of me...like luggage fit for a
Lifetime trip of pleasure wrapped in painful consequences

I TASTE you in every sip of life that I take, like bitter wine unfit to leave the vineyard

I TOUCH you and discover loving you is like running toward yesterday, missing out on
Today, and turning my back on tomorrow

I WALK AWAY FROM YOU AND THANK GOD FOR MY FIVES SENSES

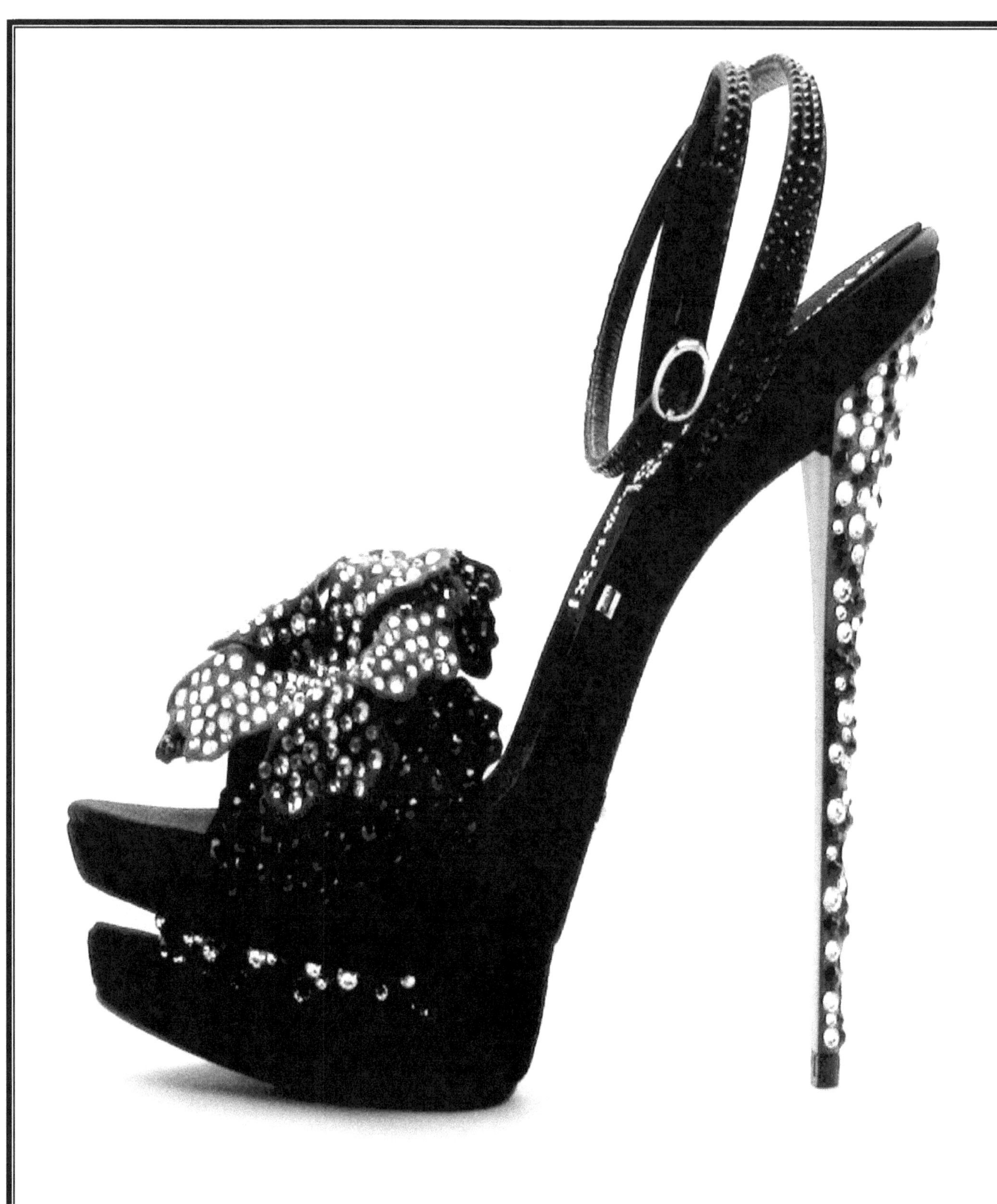

Natural Disaster

There's a HURRICANE stirring
inside of me
Someone please end this world tour
of heartache
Plaguing me like Natural
Disasters...washing away all that is
hopeful
All that it familiar
All that is comfortable

Someone please stop the torment
Remove the debris from the shell of
the woman I used to be...when our
love was EXPLOSIVE and impacted
everyone around us within arm's
reach

Someone throw me a lifeline
I'm drowning in a FLOOD of tears

Trying to make sense of when &
where the foundation we built began
to
Crack
Shake
Vibrate
Destroying our future plans like
EARTHQUAKES

Someone please stop my emotions
from spinning out of control
Tell me relief is on the way
The TORNADO of deception &
betrayal is ending
Willing to be exposed in the
aftermath

Someone please tell me I won't be
mentally buried alive in this pain
Someone please tell me...how to
survive...a broken heart

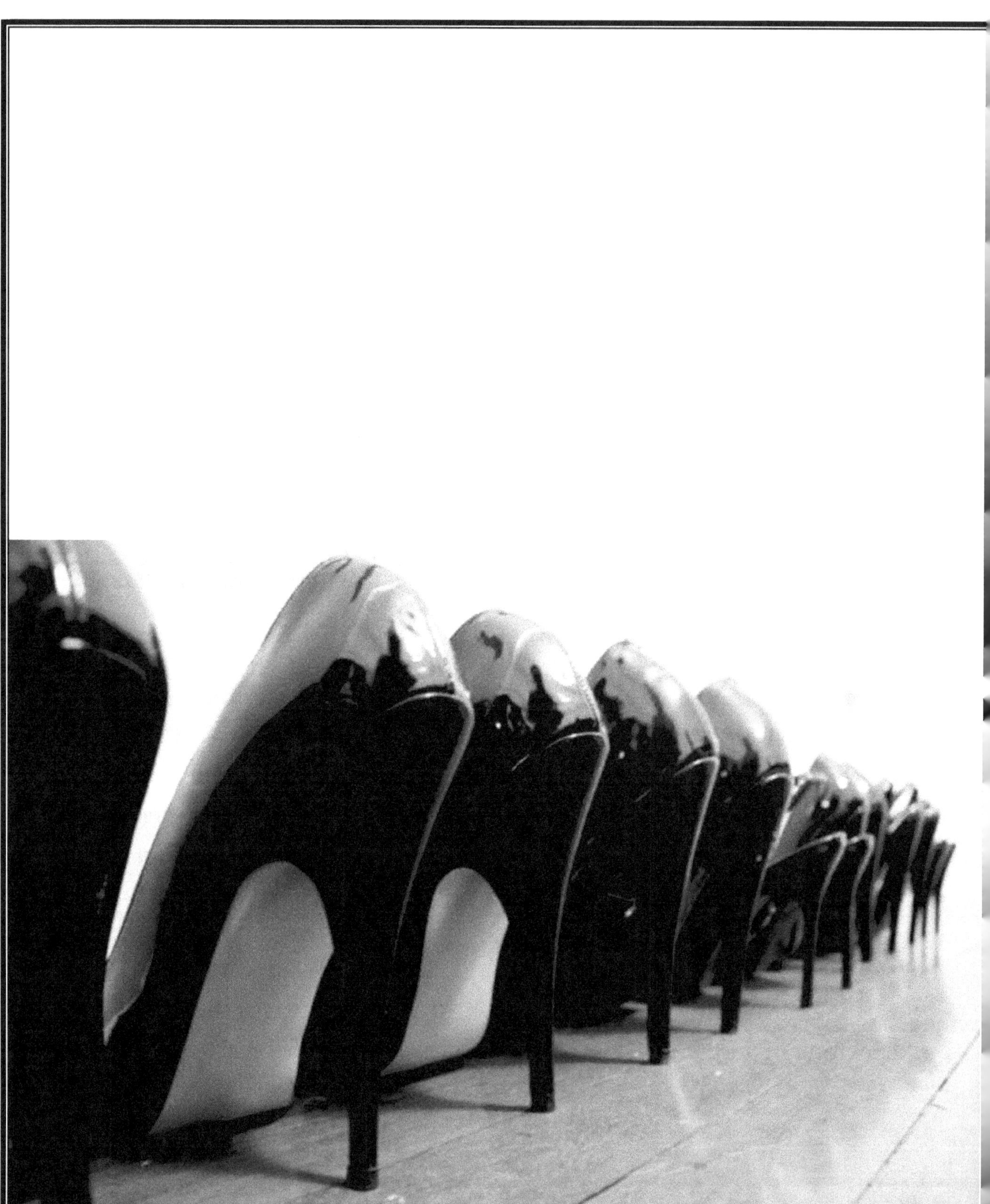

Network

How'd we meet you asked?

He'd say...we go back, but I found her on
Facebook and followed her on twitter

I'd say we reconnected on a social
networking site

I'd say he found me over long
conversations

Some profound... some pointless all
meaningful

He found me over deep silent stares and
shallow breaths...he gives me butterflies

He found me at halftime watching that
game, when I could've been watching
The Game

He found me in the heat of that
argument speaking recklessly and
reminded to speak freely yet carefully...I
found myself respectively submitting

He found me comfortably putting my
scarf on, long before taking my clothes
off
He found me somewhere between
Psalms and Proverbs

We'd say, we found one another in
friendship

What we share a status update couldn't
convey

A Twit pic couldn't capture

It takes more than a click of a button to
add or delete our connection

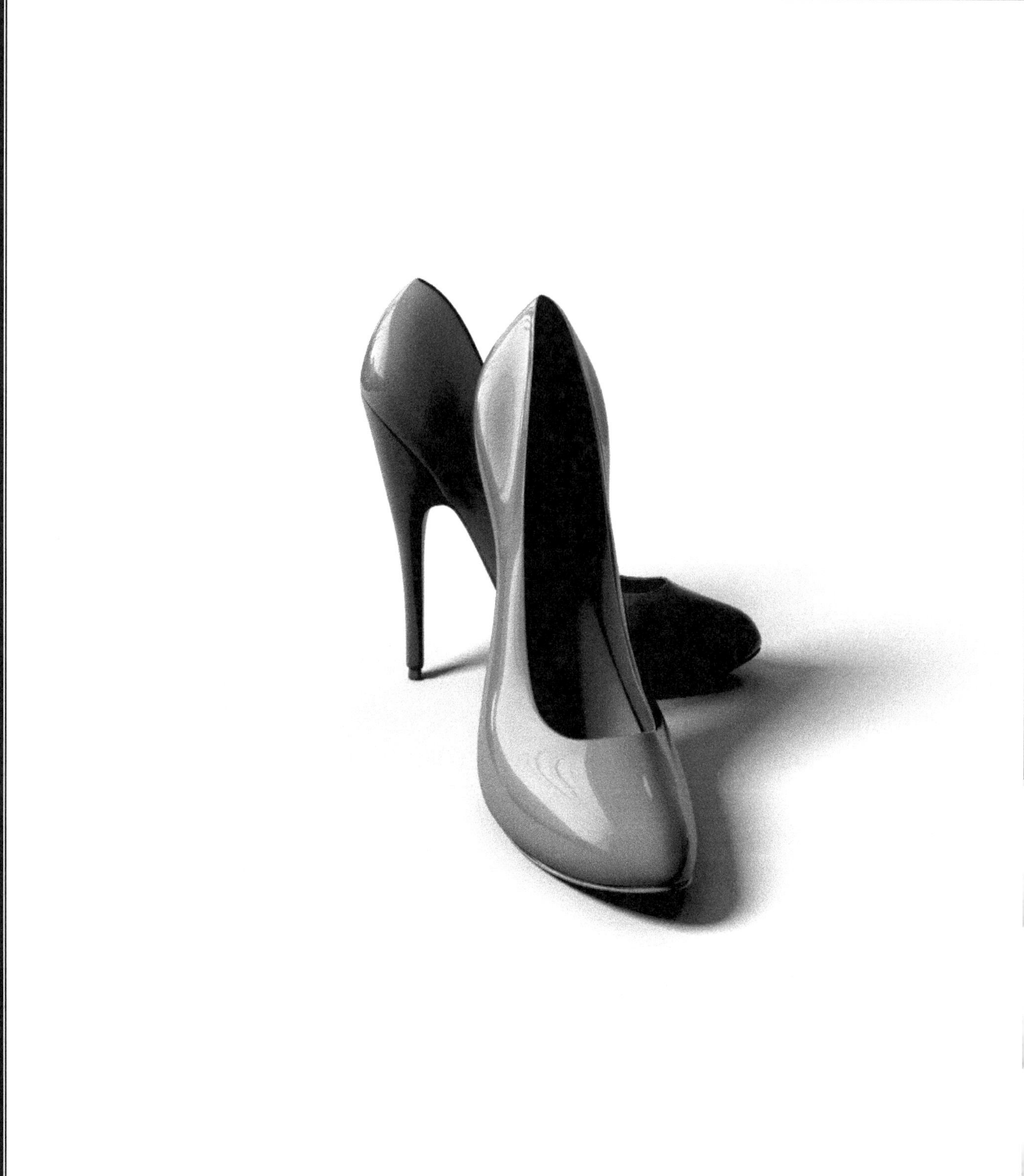

Currency

I am in control
Everyone wants me!
I've been fought over, cried for, begged for, worshiped, Prayed for...Glory

I've been in the belly of the beast and the bounty of the bosom
I've been from head to toe & hand to mouth
Been held at a high standard for a low exchange
I've been in tight spaces & done undesirable things in strange places

I've been everywhere you can imagine & places you'd only dare to dream

I've been called a lot of names

I prefer currency

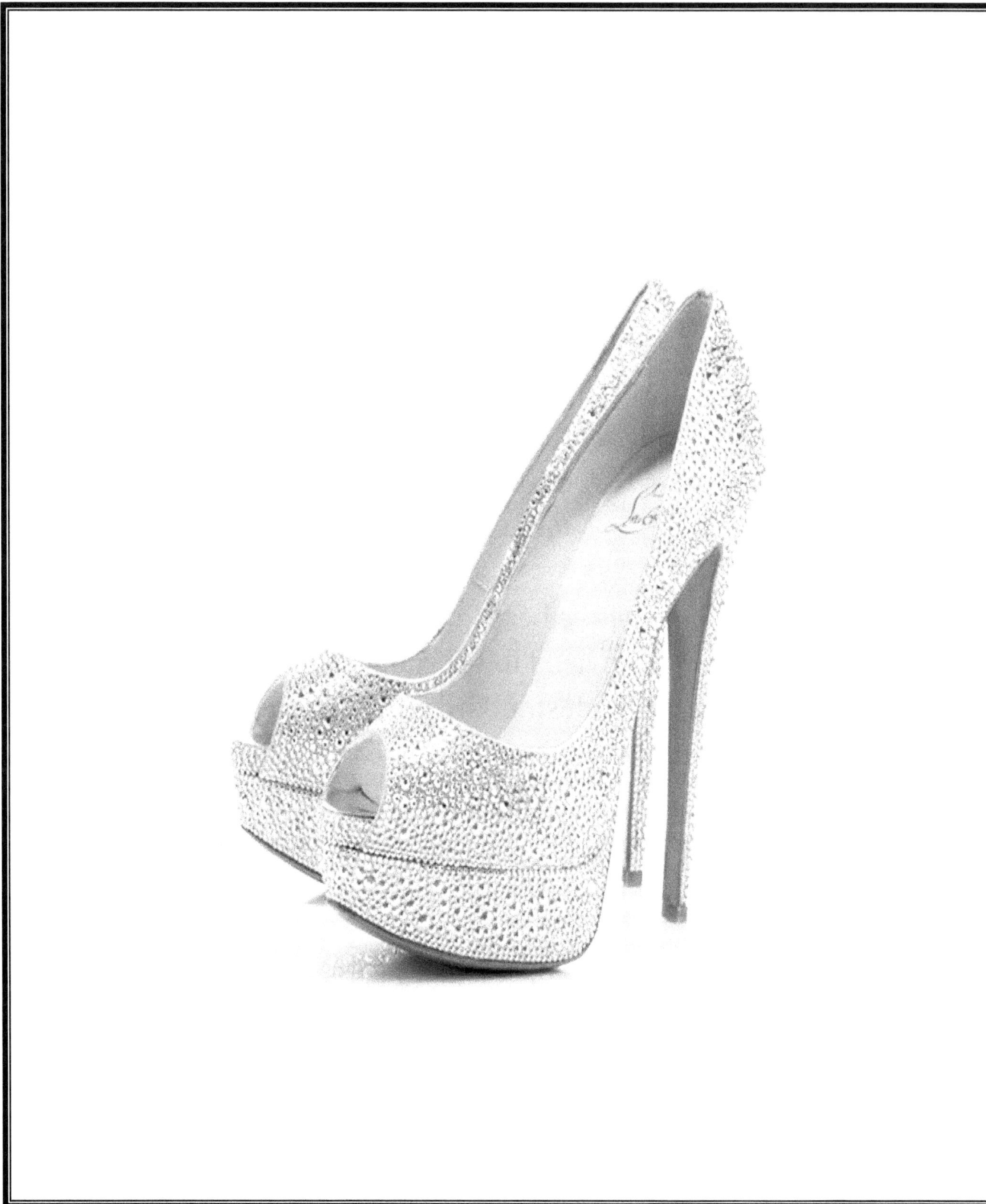

Journey of Love

I want it I need it!
What is it?

I can't touch it
I can't see it
Yet I feel compelled to believe in it
It is direct yet discreet
It is an offbeat harmony
Bitter yet so entirely sweet
It is a taste in my mouth that's unshakeable
A feeling in my heart that's unbreakable
An ache in my soul...that's painstakingly
unmistakable

It grows
It blossoms withers and dies as in the
essence of flowers
It is forever yours forever mine
With permanence that's temporarily ours
It is motionless movement as consistent as
the rhythm of an African drum
It is a volume that tranquilizes you and
leaves you numb

It's as intriguing as chocolate tides
As magical as candy coated raindrops
Splattered on sunflower sidewalks on a
warm winter day
It is those sixty seconds in every minute
Convincing you everything in love and war
is okay

What is it?

It is powerful! ... Without it life has little to
no meaning
It is free with cost
It is never for sale yet at times mistaken for
purchase
It can only be shared and or desired
It is what gives you energy yet leaves you
tired
Its form imaginable yet indescribable

It shows you everything that is or was

What is it?
It is...
This thing

This Love

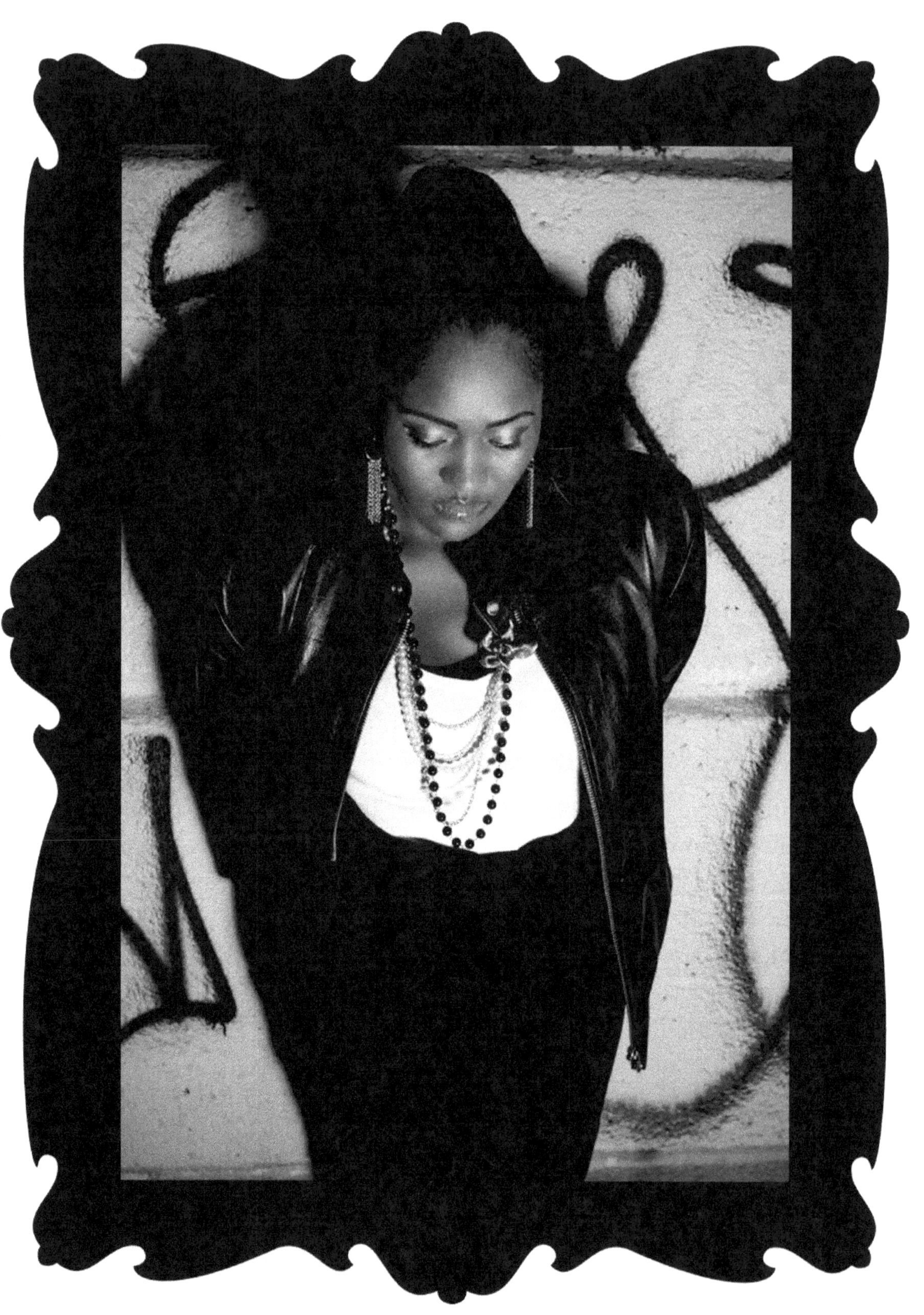

Soul Mate

I'd want to be sexual with his body, but
more importantly intimate with his mind
I'd need to know when I cry he would be
there to wipe my tears
Simply hold me while they dry
He would never offer his shoulder
Knowing I'm not one to lean
Instead he'd extend his hand and walk with
me
Through whatever chain of events life may
present

He'd know those 12 long stem red roses are
beautiful
Yet that 1 long stem black rose is
meaningful

He'd value my independence
Understand my pride
Embrace my passions
He'd trust me
Love me
Know me
Grow with me.

He'd know my Saturday nights would never
turn into Sunday mornings
Unless he and I were enjoying them
together
He'd know he'd never be my other half nor
my better half
Simply because I was born in completion
therefore I'm whole

He'd know it would never be his
responsibility to make me happy nor mine
to make him happy
We could only contribute to each other's
happiness

He'd know for as strong as I am
I'm even more delicate

He'd know how much I adore butterflies in
my stomach & work at keeping them there

Shakina

Lewis

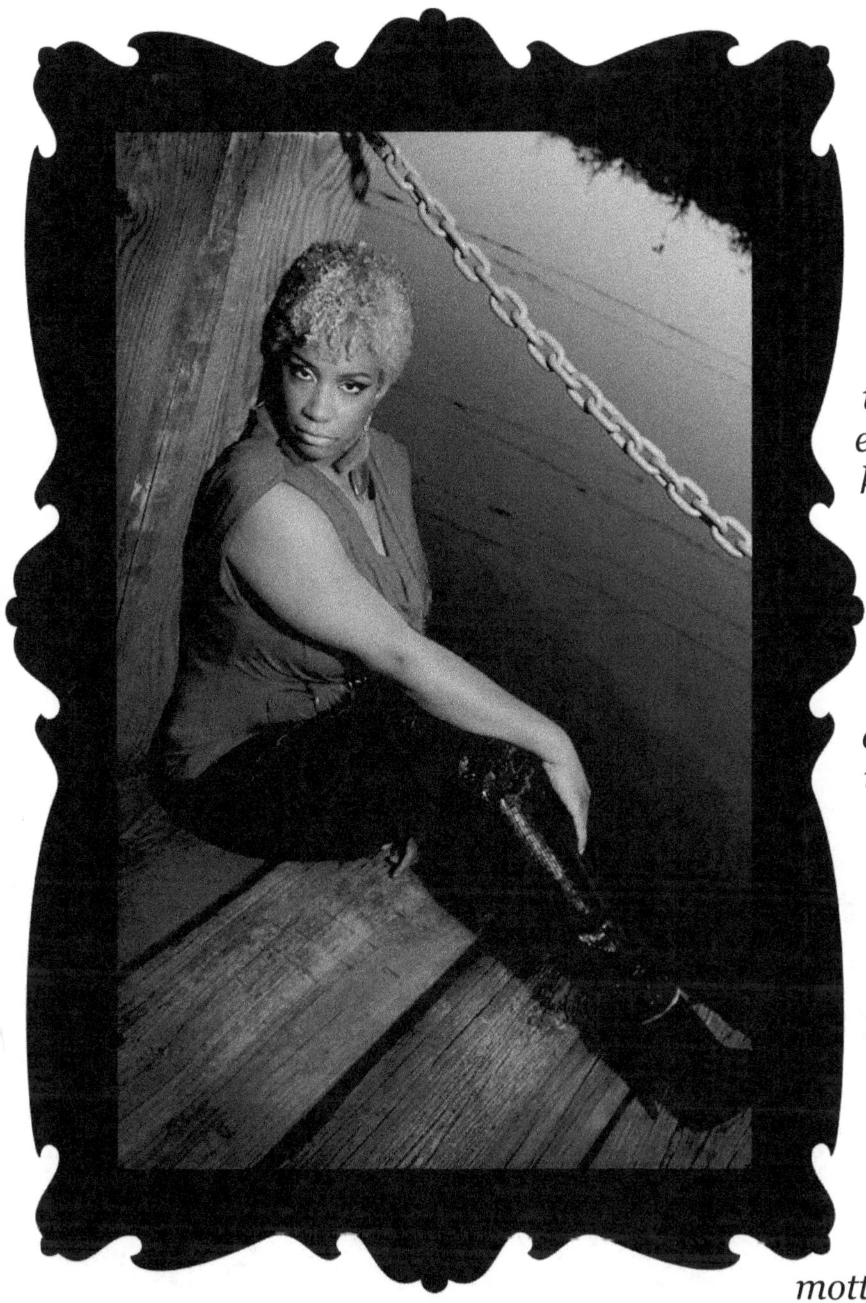

"Walk, Talk, and Live Success I'm better than blessed because I am blessed by the best." Is one of my favorite things to say! I started writing at the age of eight years old to break out from underneath life struggles I endured as a child. Who knew that someone like me would grow up to one day be able to share my poetry with the world. I first started out as a spoken word artist in my early 20s. To transfer my words of the paper and bring them alive on stage was a high I could I not elucidate. One of greatest gifts God has given me is to bring healing to others through my words. My sorrows, my laughter, the abuse and my insecurities became a stepping stone into my purpose. So I pray as you read my poems and mottos you will see my past, my present and my future. My poetry purpose is clear; to convict hearts, convince minds and touch souls for Christ. Be blessed by my thoughts...

♥*Kina*

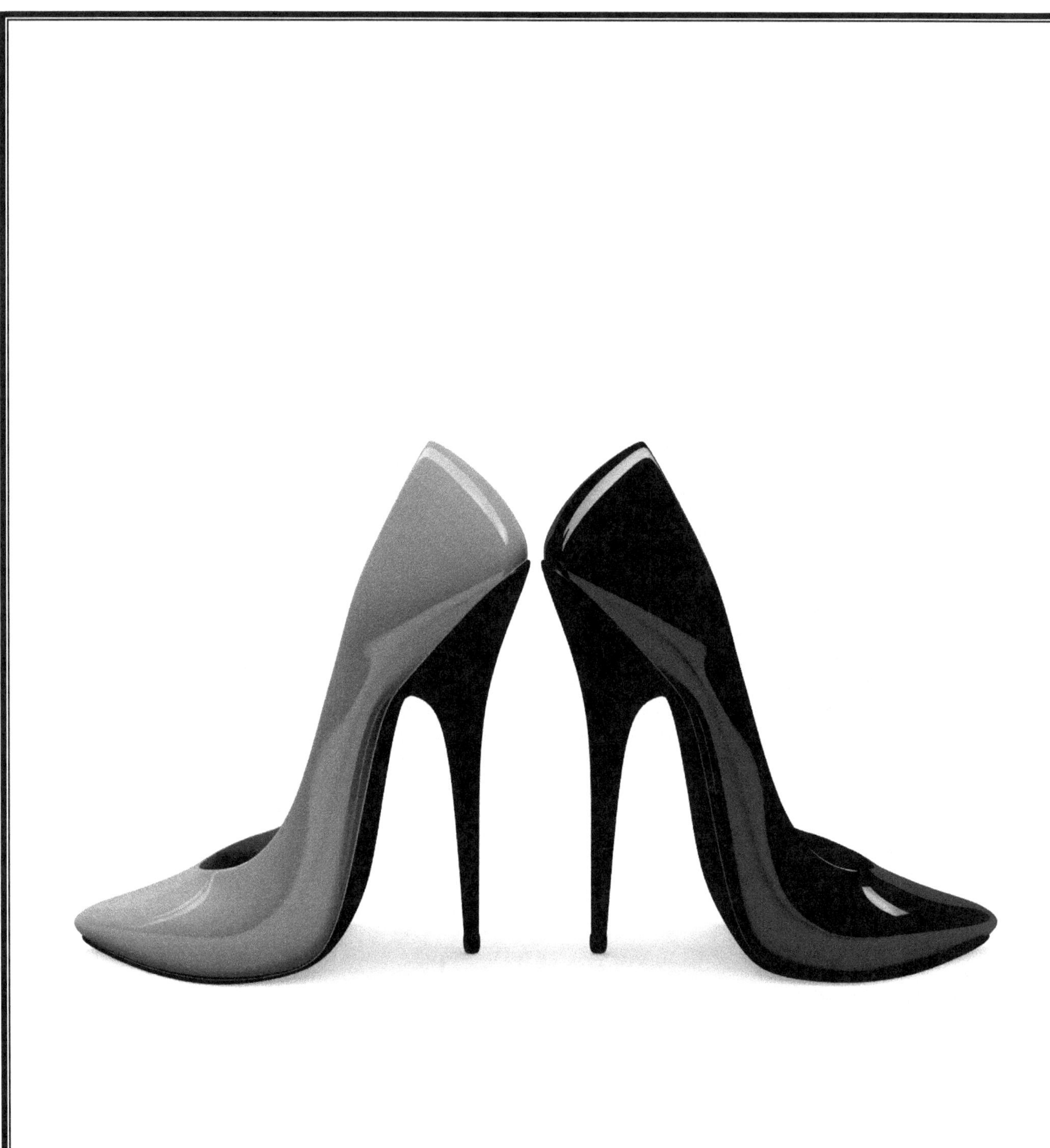

Texture of Hair

I ought to care
About the texture of my hair
On any given day
Should my hairstyle give it away
Being the woman I portray
I bought into the lye
That I was prettier with a bang
That covers my eyes
Girls with long hair and cute faces
Were destined to go places
As my mother struggled to part my hair
That was curly and too thick for a comb
Was forced to stay home
So I wouldn't sweat out my curls
Since a young girl, she would say
A woman should never have a BAD hair day
Her hair is her glory
Each strand tells a story
Curly, coarse, thick or "kinky" afro hair
Straight, fine or even *fair*
Long, short or even bald
Encouraging all
To stand tall
Permed, relaxed and dyed
Dry scalp and spilt ends
What matters is what's within
Went from a jerry curl
To shaved off in the back
Later on that wasn't enough
Went all natural with my afro puff
Now I'm blonde and I had to go hairless
So I can be careless
Sometimes I have to fight so my voice can be heard
Petite, light skin and almost bald is absurd
In a world that tells little girls
That artificial hair is better than your natural curls
Longer is better and prettier if it's straight
It's better to buy hair instead of keeping your natural state
Must the texture of my hair define my social role?
My place in society
Does my hair have that much control?
I am more than what is on top of my head
What comes out of my soul should matter instead
I'm more than a fantasy for men's eyes to see
More than a tool in the bedroom when he's ready to release
More than an image they portray on TV
I'm more than just hair
It's me that stands underneath

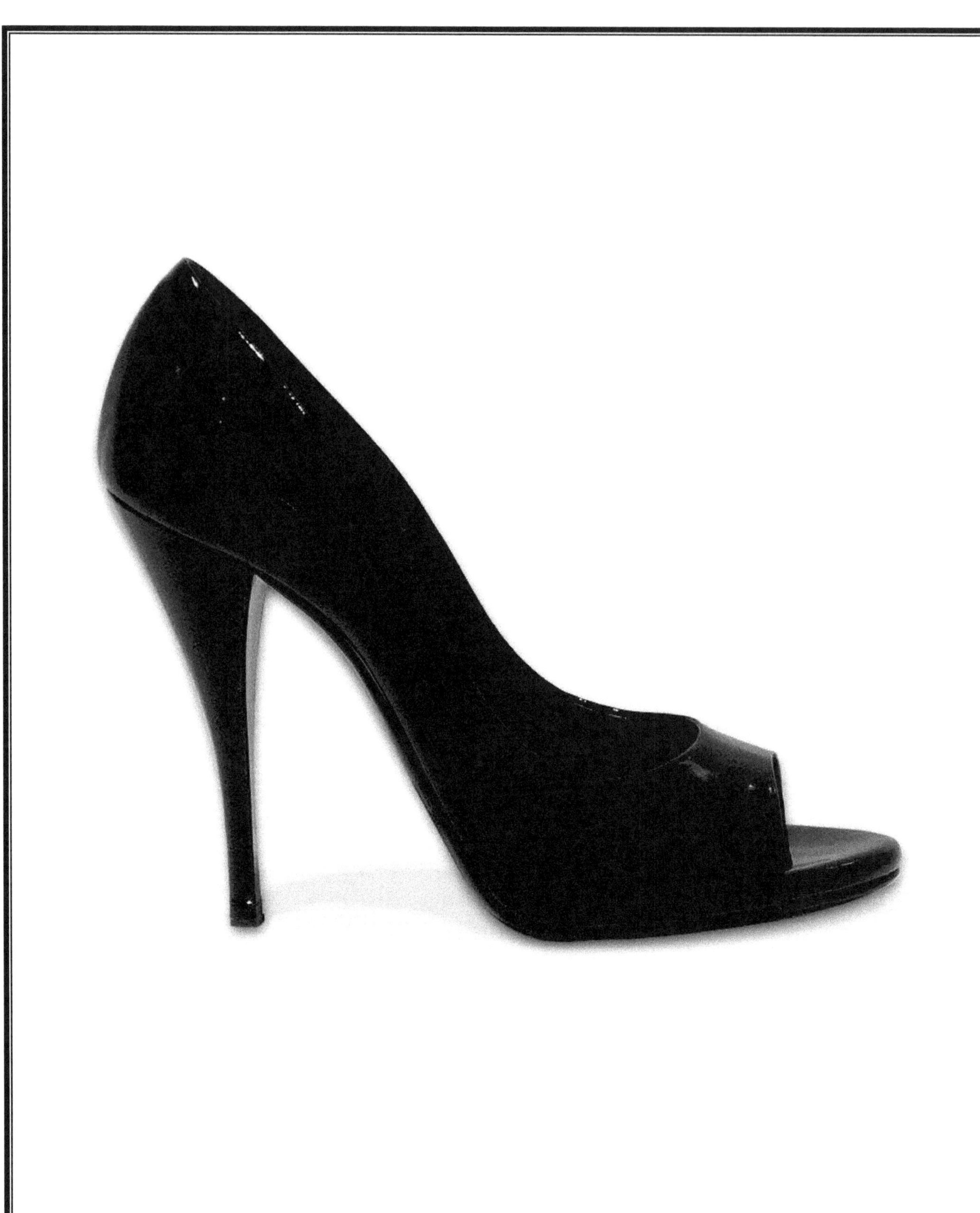

As Often

As often as the wind blows
That's how quickly a life is taken
Young and aged many lives have been forsaken
As often as the street lights change
From red to green
A mile away is police sirens
Rushing to crime a scene

As often as a infant is born
Funerals homes are filled with mothers who mourn
As often as a woman shampoos her hair
Children are being abuse while in childcare
As often as a vehicle needs fuel
Twenty percent of our youth dropped out of school

As often as it takes to read one line
Every eight second cigarettes causes someone to die
As often as the sun set
Mistakes are being made that many regret
As often as ships sail
Someone is taken to jail

No matter how often these things maybe
I'll write often to decrease
The unspoken woes of this world
Until often melts into seldom

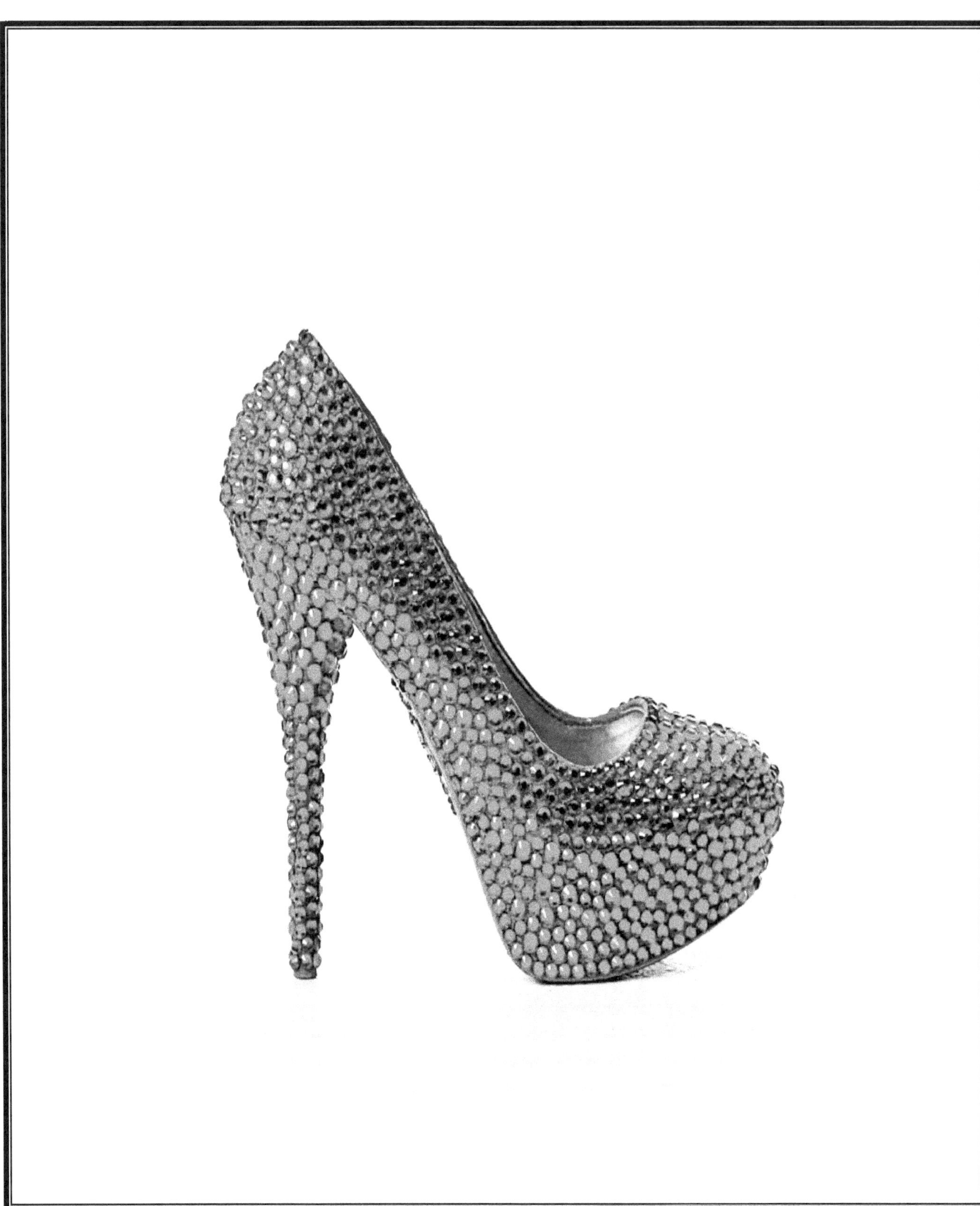

HARD BUT; WORTH IT

I was seventeen and pregnant
My pride and arrogance
Made me to believe
This could never happen to me
See, I knew I was beautiful
But too grown
For my own good
Thought my looks would
Be a way out of the hood
Instead of making good grades
I majored in the trade
Being fine and the different methods of birth control
As I thought I understood
I had dreams, like many girls
With pretty faces
But lack of self-esteem
Caught up in the schemes
Having life goals was just a daydream
It was hard but worth it
To finish high school
With a baby on board
Neither job nor higher education
How could I afford
Its was hard but worth it
To learn how to love someone other than myself
No proper role model of a mother
Had to put my dreams on a shelf
Hard but worth it
To work and take care of child
Go back to school
All the while I smile
Refuse for them to see me sweat
It was hard but worth it
To fight off threats
I'm nothing more than a hood-rat
It was hard but worth it
To show them otherwise
Bought my first home at twenty five
It was hard but worth it
To earn my degree
Raise, not one child but three
It was hard but worth it
To move on after my divorce
And looking back I have no remorse
It was hard but worth it
To confront my issues
To make a change
As systems and people stayed the same
It may get hard but you are worth it

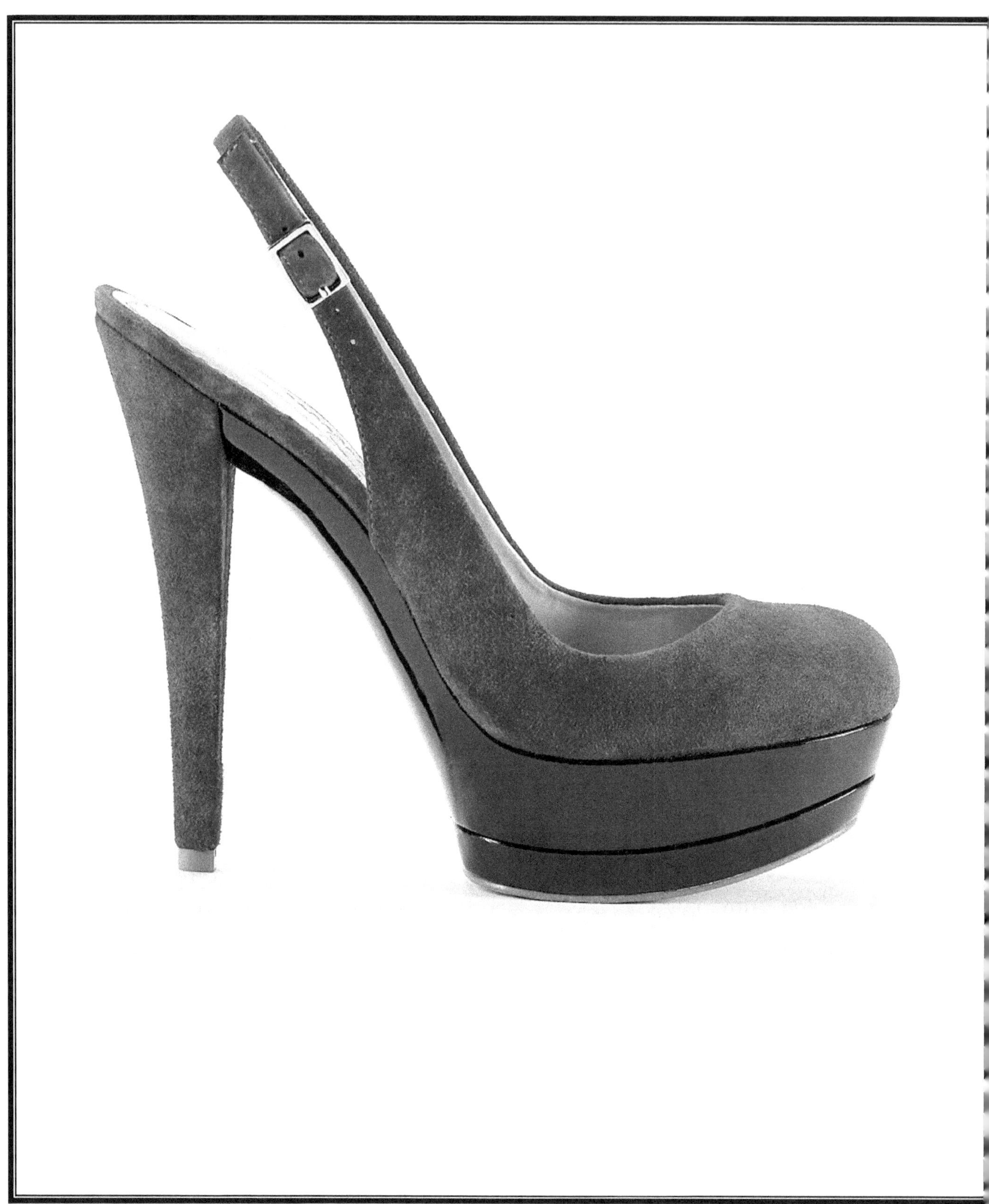

He's Mine

He makes love to my emotions
Caress my intellect
And seduce my mentality
Indulging the little girl inside of me
He makes me laugh when I ought to cry
Times I feel like giving up
He urges me to try
He's intimate beyond the sheets
Get chills whenever we meet
His strokes feel like a cup of warm tea
On a chilly night
Love watching horror flicks
Give me a reason to hold him tight
I can tell him everything that's on the hush-hush
Then he tickles my neck and makes me blush
He's my man
Understand me better than my girlfriend can
When I'm in the wrong
He speak the truth in love
He's gentle but strong
Caring but firm
Daring but careful
No doubt he's for me
I have all the signs
He was meant to me mine

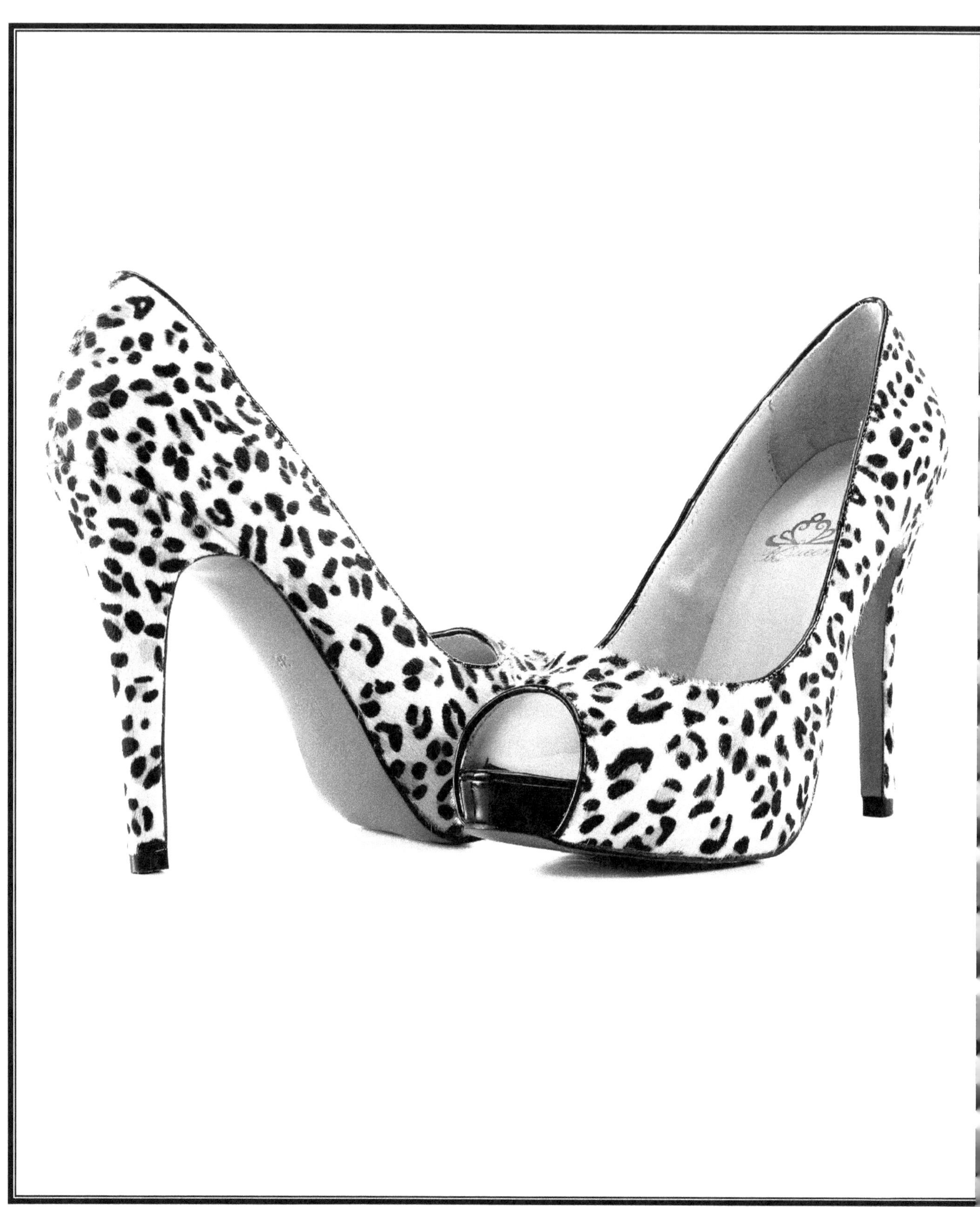

WHY I WRITE

Poetry is more than a pastime
More than a figure of speech that rhymes
Just to hear the audience go OH or AWW
It doesn't hurt to hear it once in awhile
Laugh out loud
My poetry is a mouthful of air; Walking among flesh giving hope to the listener's ear
My expressions do more than entertain
Great slogans in a commercial for ad campaigns
I'm not known for writing fairytales
But I write against the depths of hell
Writing against all inhumanity
Hoping that my endeavors won't be in vain
Why do I write?
I'm glad you ask
I write to unmask
How young girls master the trade
Of pleasuring little boys with Blowjobs before the 7th grade
Being popular is more important than self-respect
If the problems continues to go unchecked
School aged girls will cry more about cramps in their necks.
Eager to finish all homework for Sex Ed
But failing, reading and math instead
Little boys acting like a lawyer in a courtroom
Their opening statement
"Shorty can I hit?"
Your honor I object
You not ready for sex
Not even old enough to get a work permit
Kids having sex before they can drive
On the highway of love with no seatbelts
That's why many don't survive
For a lack of better words
They are rushing to get it in
Like a fast food meal
If it's not cooked
You will get ill
Girls as young as ten
On birth control
Remembering to take their pill
Becomes their long-term goal
Some parents have to work more than one job
To make ends meet
While Society has a failed to provide a place
To keep our kids off the streets
Why do I write?
I'm glad you ask
I write to save the future
As I expose my past

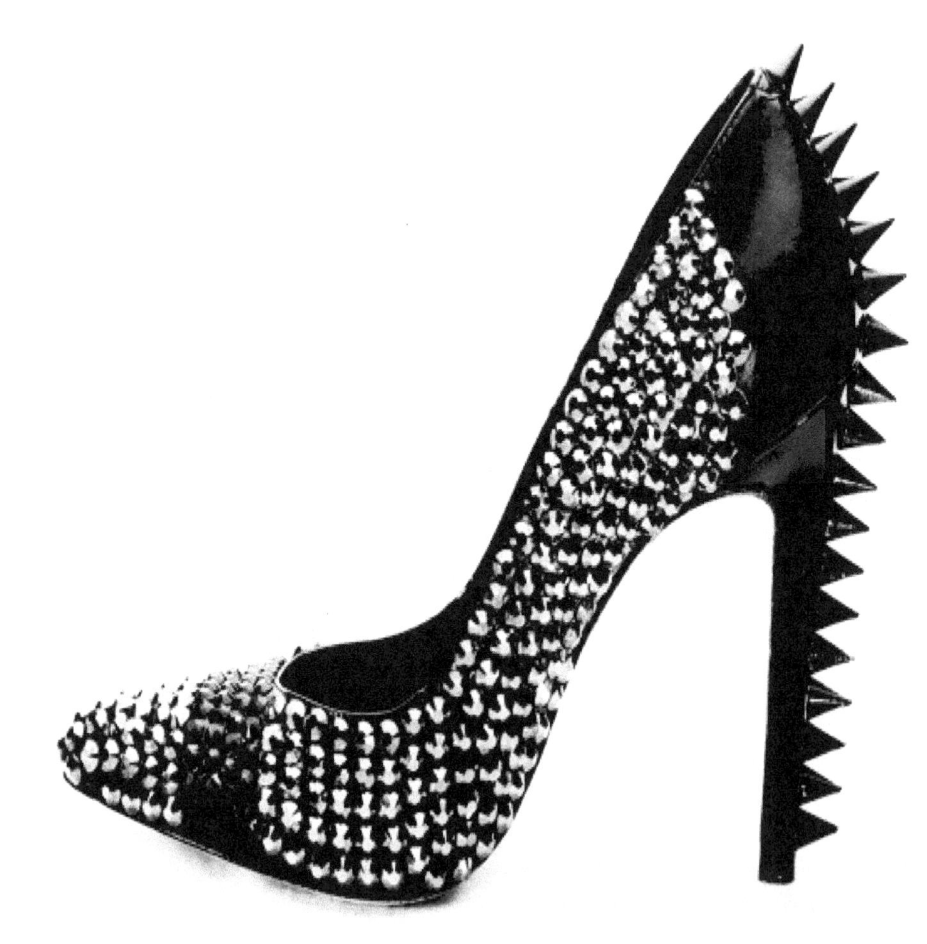

The Job of a People Pleaser

Giving more
Than, What I ever get
Feeling like
I'm always at the
The shorter end of the stick
Lost more than
What I gained
Caring for others
While engorging
My own pain
Cried more than laugh
Without any pay
I became the service staff
Of everyone's well being
I got no days off
Nor time and a half
No time for me
Even to enjoy a hot bath
I made it my business
To become, the
CEO of others affairs
No retirement fund
Or investment shares
I was the personal assistant
Of their tears
Their problems were my employer
And every offense
I acted as their defense lawyer
My schedule was booked
With the events of others needs
Because I aimed to please
No sick leave
Or vacation days
No bonuses
No raise
I received
No Pats on the back
And praises of, thank you
I needed that
At the end of the day
Feeling like someone's doormat
I was drained and worn out
And for, my needs
I went without
Now
The journey begins
I see
There's only one
I need to please

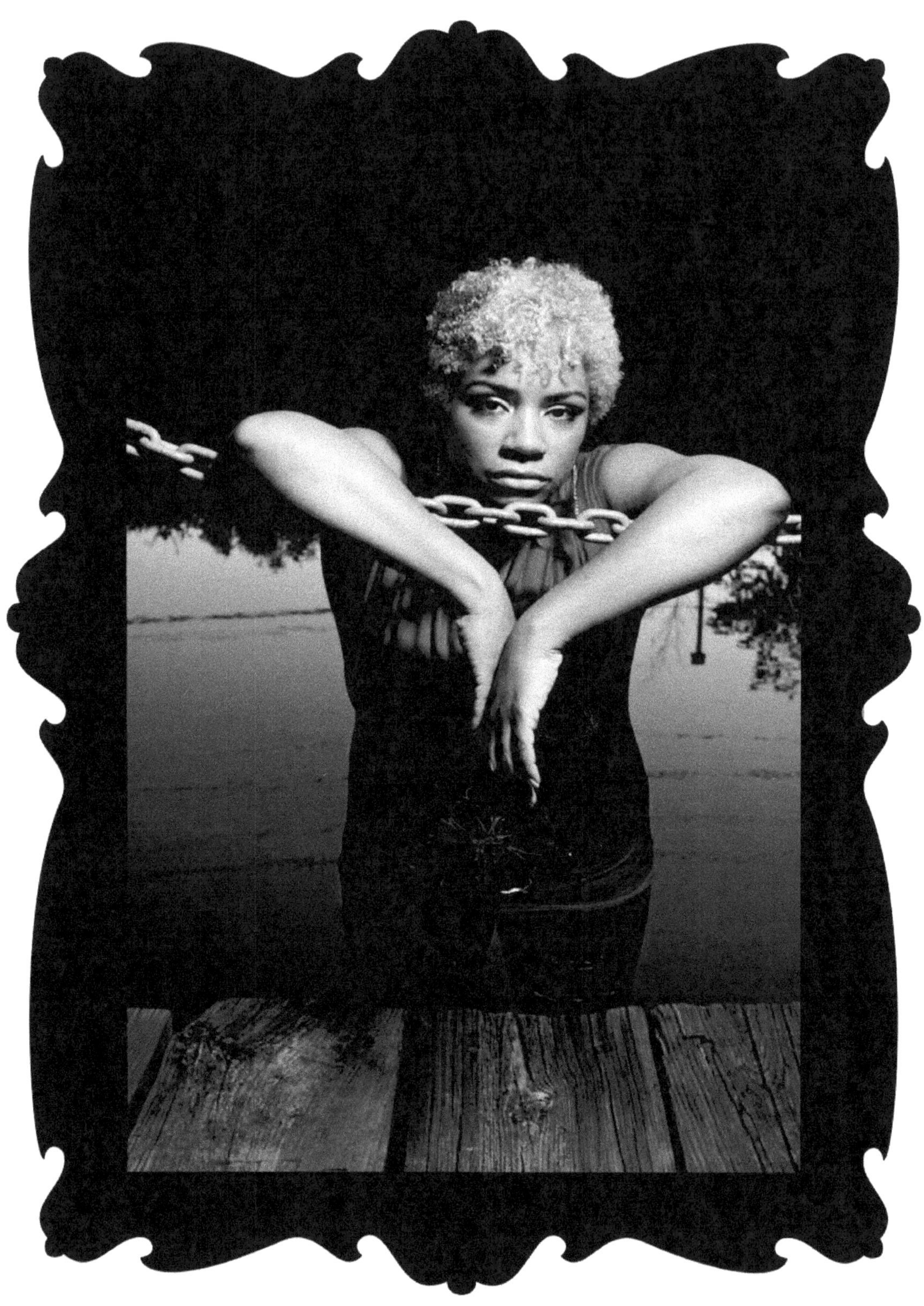

Shout Out

I need to give out a shout out
To these young girls
Who have it hard
Living in this crazy world
I know things are ruff
Dealing with a lot of stuff
But hang in there
Don't give up

This right here is for them girls
Who moms a druggie
She's left at home with no love
Her man comes by
Too old to be a thug
Playing daddy giving fake hugs
She prays all night for her mom
To get well

People are shocked
You rebelled
Mom can't get the things you need
Instead she gets high off weed
Don't blame your self
Instead take heed
Don't lose your hope
With God you will succeed

Girls with daddies bedding more than one lover
Playing daddy at home but in the street he's a pimp undercover
Because he has children with more than one significant other

Now he tells you to stay away from sex
Don't want boys to call
But he's in the club doing free for all

Daddy's never home
So he don't understand
Why you run into the arms of another man

At a young age
It's sex you adage
Girlfriend don't disrespect your self
I was in your shoes
You can choose
To take God's help

Made a mistake
Baby out of wedlock
I can relate
Responsibility to hard to take
Looking for a way out
But can't get a break

In and out the system
Trying to survive
Father no help cause he claims it's not mines

You going school part time
To earn your degree
Friends & family tripping saying
Who is she?

All you want is better
For you and baby
You think they'll agree

Young mother keep your head up
God can do it for you
Like he did it for me

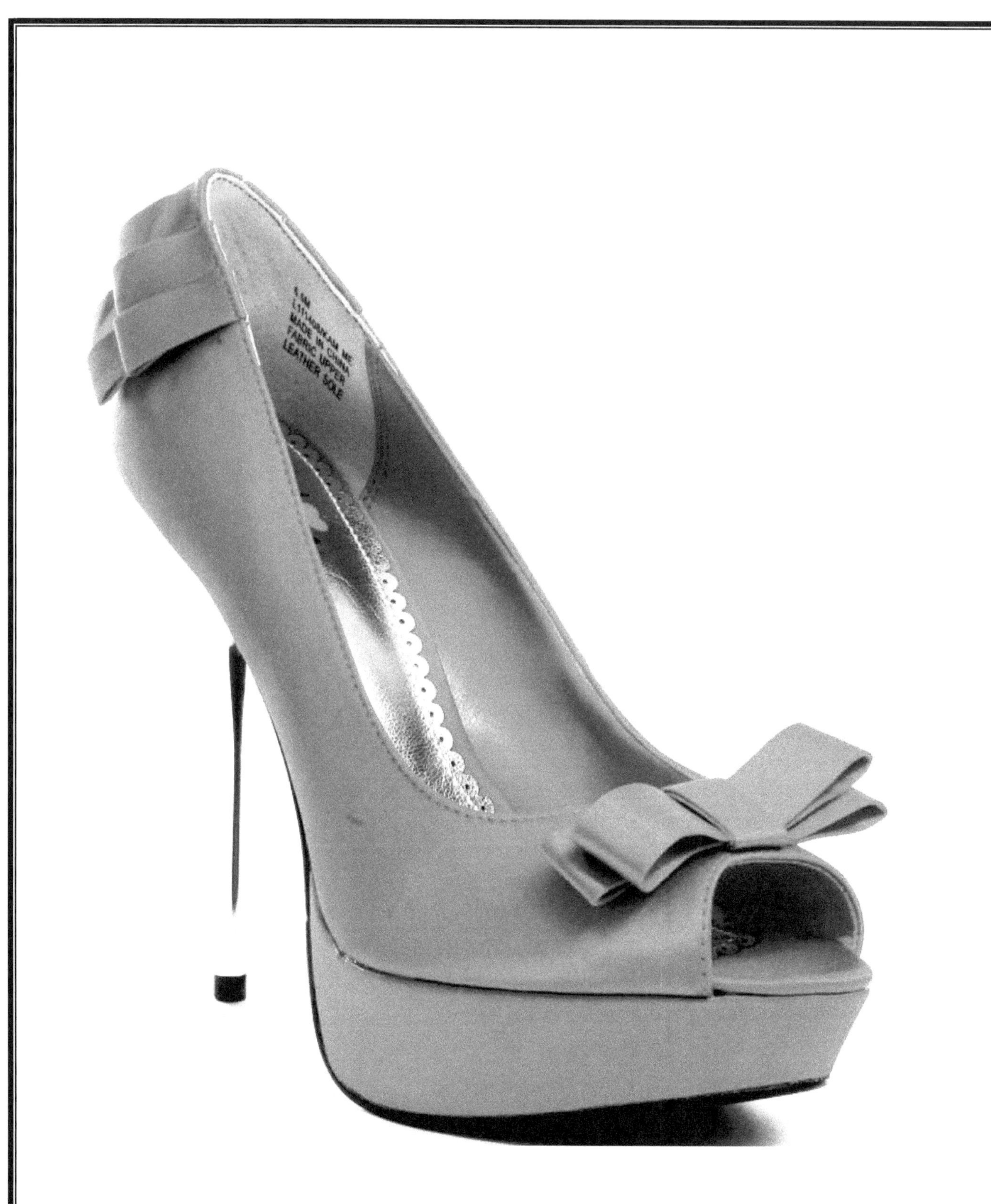
MADE IN CHINA
FABRIC UPPER
LEATHER SOLE

Shoe Sale

One day I'm at the mall
And mad about how I couldn't find
Anything at all
I'm not like many women
That loves to shop
I want to be in
And out without
Making additional stops

Scuffling in my purse looking for my keys
I turned my head
And I see
Shoe sale with 40% percent off
Staring back at me

They had boots
From pumps to open toes shoes
They had every style to every color
How could one choose?

During these economic times
This was a steal
What woman in her right mind
Don't like a deal?

I took a bold step
And approached the sale person
I asked is this really true?
Yes she said "how may I help you"

I said, I need shoes for work, church and play
I need a pair in neutral colors; for everyday
She took me towards the back
Never saw so many shoes on one rack

Honestly, I thought
I don't need new shoes
But who can pass up a sale
Would you?
And there they were
Wedge heels as I prefer
Black, with red and white zebra stripes
Perfect for a dress or either tights
Thinking to myself, all I need is my size
"Excuse me Ms.
Do you have an 8 and half for me to try?"
"Yes we do" she replied
As I took the shoes to wear
I thought all my friends who will wish
They had a pair
Walked up to cashier
While grinning from ear to ear

Pulled out my card to pay
Noticed I had no more money
And the sale ends after today
I asked the manager can he put these shoes on hold
No I was told
But I'll be right back
No he said they will go back on the rack

I stood there and thought
All of this for some shoes
Rubbing my forehead looking confused

See I didn't want to use
My credit card I just refuse!

Only a second to make up my mind
People behind me upset while
I'm holding up the line
As hard as it was
I gave the shoes back
I watched them put them back on the rack
Felt sorry that I wasn't prepared
For the biggest shoe sale of the year
What a lesson to learn
Always be prepared when it's your turn

Better decisions and planning ahead
Living on purpose and in purpose
Today a shoe sale
Tomorrow life

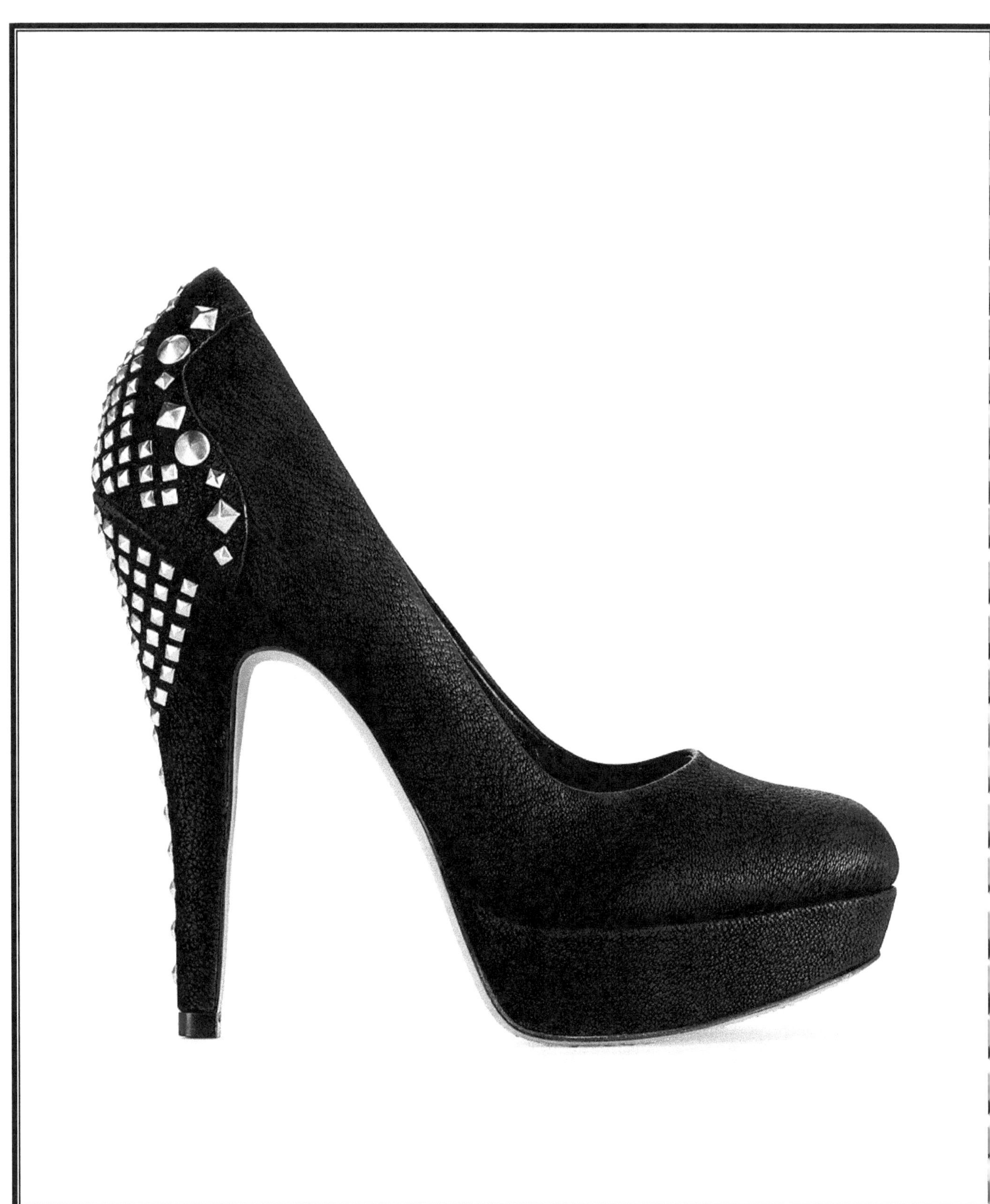

PRISON BARS

I felt sometimes that life
Was like the prison system
That held me in contempt of court
Of bad situations and a rap sheet
Of negative reports
I didn't know my rights
So I remained a good sport
I never stepped foot in a jail
But my environment was like a prison cell
And there was no bail
No way of breaking free
Of generational curses
That plagued me
Why try to pursue
Anything, when history as I knew
Had a long list
Of what I couldn't do
Who are you? I heard
From those who preferred
Cried constantly, why me
No success to break free
Made many appeals
Hoping life would just cut them a deal
There was no easy way out
Just got tired of living without
I'm ready to close my case
Instead of fighting life, I begin to embrace
Breaking free
From the prison blocks
Of bad decisions
Breaking free
From chain locks
Of dire relationships and religion
Breaking free
From past hurts and pains
A lot was lost but much to gain
I have the right to remain silent
But I choose to speak
Or forever will I hold my peace
I'm breaking free
From life's prison system
Will you join me?

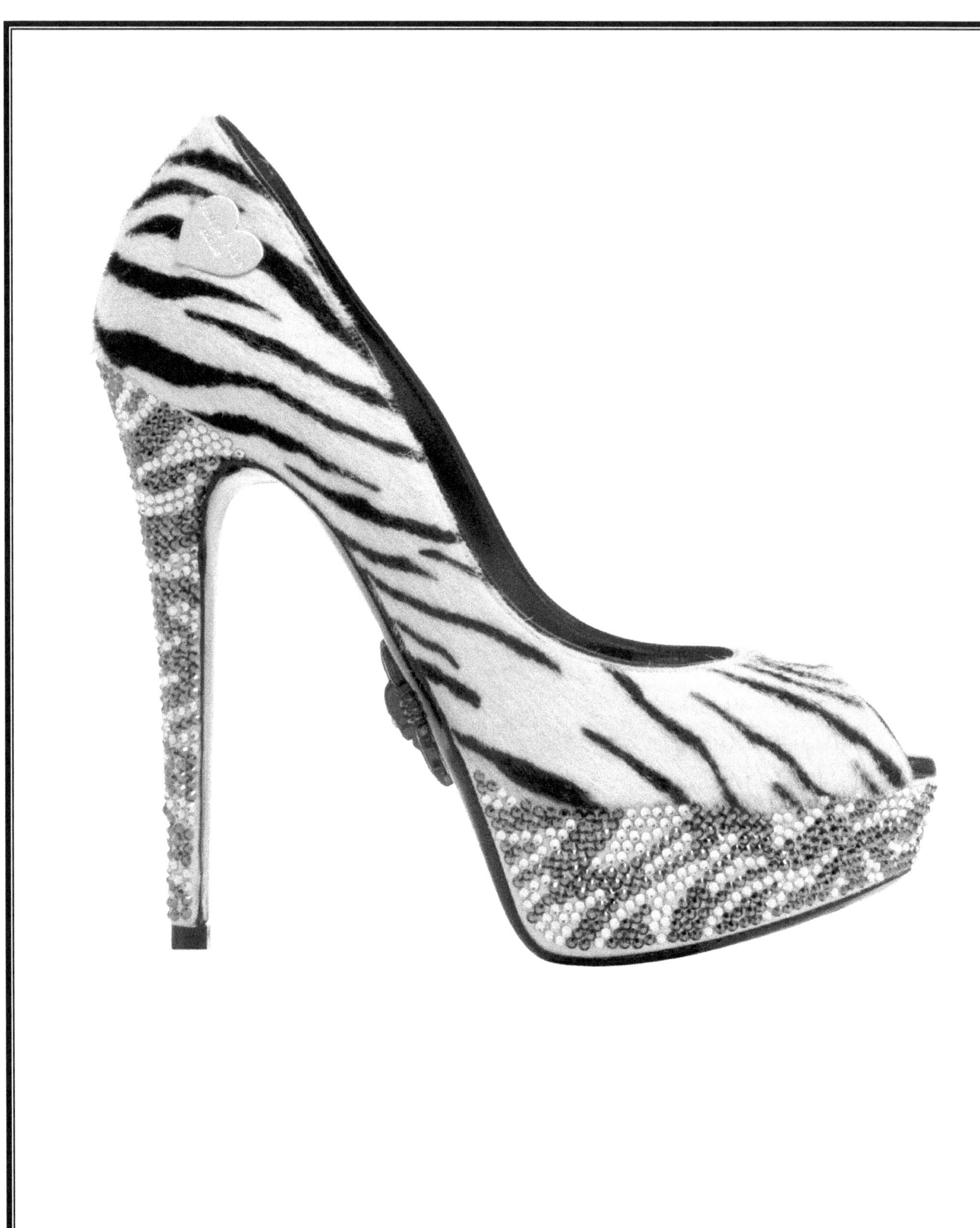

No More,

I Won't Relive My Past

"Move forward because theirs nothing in the past; worth looking forward to"

No more living in pang of guilt
Took many years to rebuild
All that been lost
The cost of my cross
Was only for me to bear
My tears were liquid prayers
Me, they tried to harass
The historical events of my past

But here today with no sorrow
Proclaiming freedom for my tomorrow

Nix, being in the background anymore
Have too much in store
Got my wings and ready to fly
Waving bye to every lie
Whispered about me
Its time to change my mind
No fault to others for my state of being
Not living by folks terms
Today I reaffirm
Finding my own voice
Making a choice
To succeed

Above my own expectations
Without any limitations

Seized back my power
Won't waste another hour
Feeling less than
Standing on His promises
So I can, now shine

I won't be pushed back in line
Won't be used for others pleasures
Won't compare my success
By their measures

Won't live in the gloom
Concerning what someone assumes

Won't relive my past
Thank God I'm free at last
Learned from my before
Pressing toward my future
As I soar

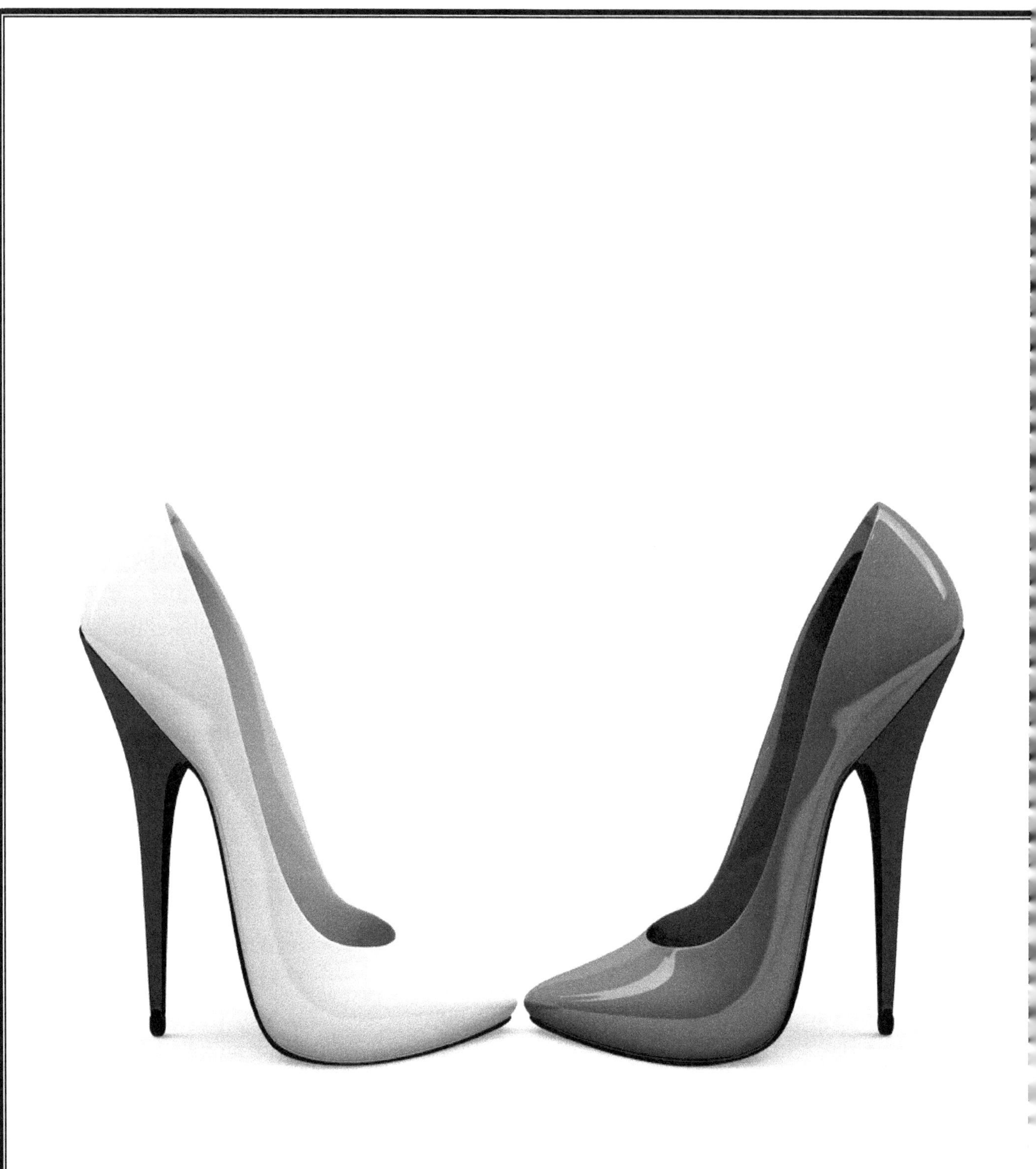

Life as a Movie

My life like a movie
People hurried to stand in line
My name is lights on a large advertisement sign
Waiting to see me on the big screen
The light goes out
The credits begin
They sit on the edge of their seats
Anticipating the end
Amazed to see
All that I went through
To be me
So in return I say
Let God make a movie out of you today
Live your destiny
No edits needed

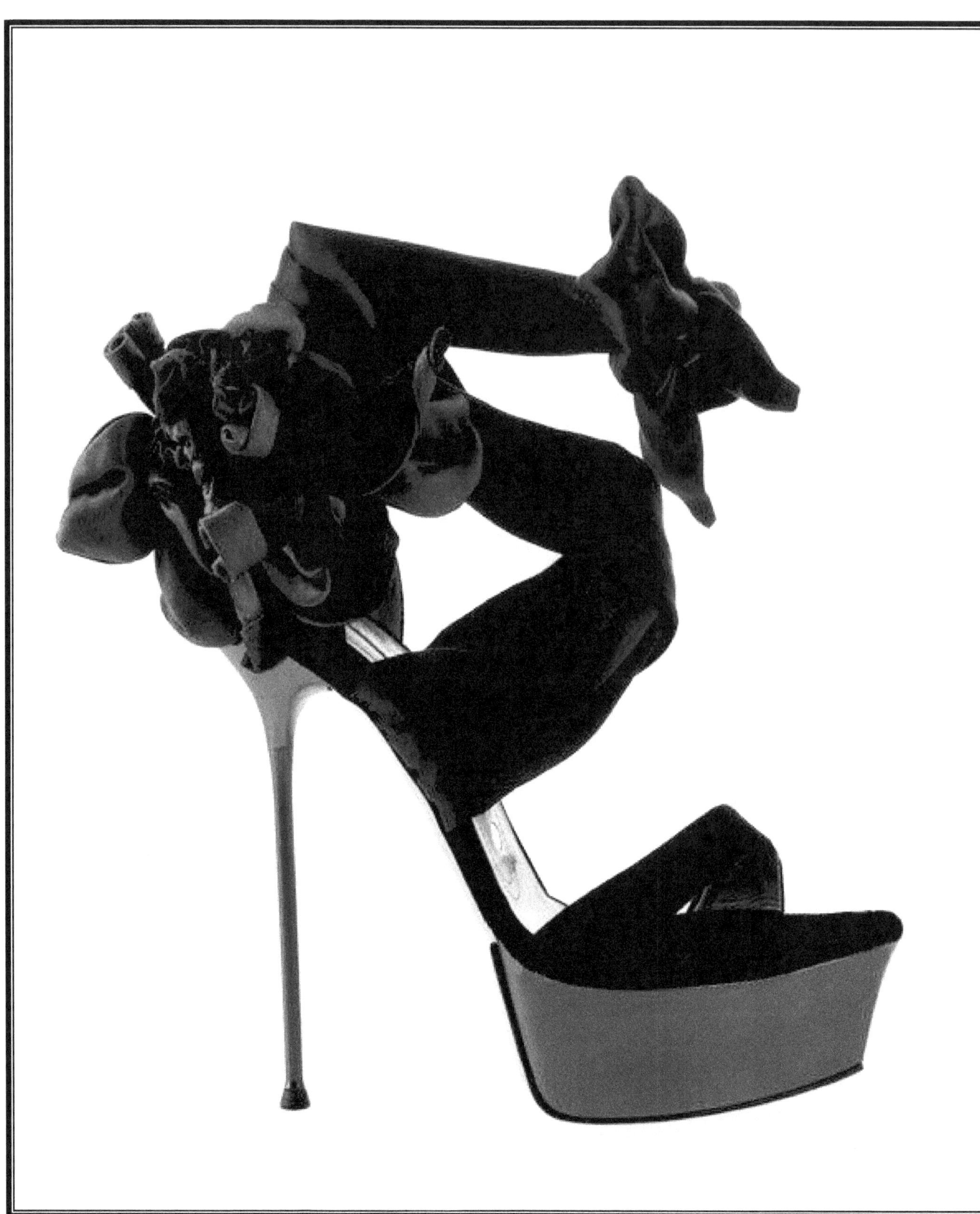

If I Was

If I was an RB song
I would be listed on the top ten
Of the charts
If I was a portrait
I would be known as a work of art
Not to brag or boast
But I'm not the least of them
I'm the most
If I was a perfume
I'll be Chanel No. 5
If I was an automobile
Everyone would want a ride
If I was left in the wilderness
I would be one to survive
If I was a star
I would shine
I would stay on everyone's mind
From my thoughts
My desires
My full lips causing four alarm fires
My Hair
To my stare
I'm one of a kind
Embracing the woman I am today
Celebrating the woman of yesterday
One experience at a time

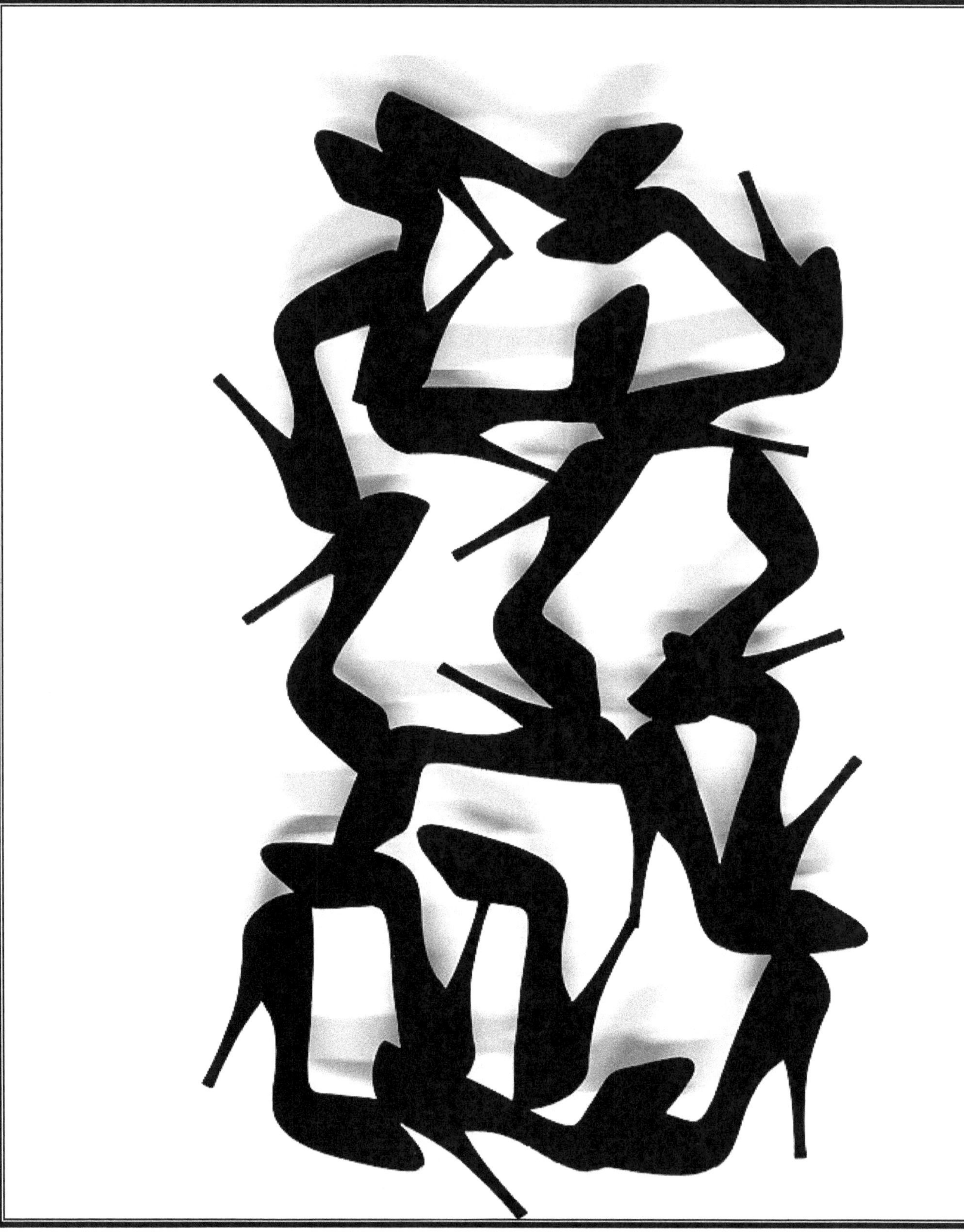

Only One of Me

When I go a restaurant, I dislike when someone eats off my plate without my permission. They are so worry about what's on everyone else plate without eating their own food. Sometimes in the body of Christ there is jealously and backbiting. We can get so concern about what someone else is doing and this will distract us from what God has for us. Eat off the plate God has made for you.

Why, bring up my past?
Harsh words,
Said against me,
Shall not last
See, that was me, then
But this is now
Nor, will I allow
Depressing sounds,
To keep me confound.

Why, remind me
Of who I use to be?
I know you see,
How God has set me free
Do you know?
What I had to go through
To see what stands before you.

What's the point
Of throwing my faults in my face?
Is it to make me feel?
Ashamed and disgrace
Why should I take that in?
Jesus Christ already died for my sin

Why talk behind my back?
To Sister Mary, usher Sue and Dec Jack.
About my transgressing and what I lack.
Face the facts, you are not all that.

Why the need?
To see me fall
Blather, she nothing at all.
Hoping I'll fall on my face.
Tripping me up,
We are running the same race.
Pressing on
To get in, that great place.
To the Kingdom of God
Home where we shall dwell
I am not concern about you?
You don't have,
A Heaven or Hell.
To put me in

Why?
Criticizing every little thing I do?
From the way I walk, talk and dress.
Who are you?
To judge me
And my ways
To say I am not godly
Cause, I chose not to where white
On communion Sunday

Point is,
I 'm no different than you.
I have trail and tribulations I gone through.
God gives me,
Peace of mind
To know He's working it out
In His Divine Time

No need to be jealous,
Of what I become.
Jesus Christ did it for me,
He can do it for anyone.
Fix your mind to be more like him.
The only Begotten Son

So, please don't envy my gifts, talents and abilities.
It's useless
It's like chasing the wind.

Why,
Because there's Only One of Me
Amen.

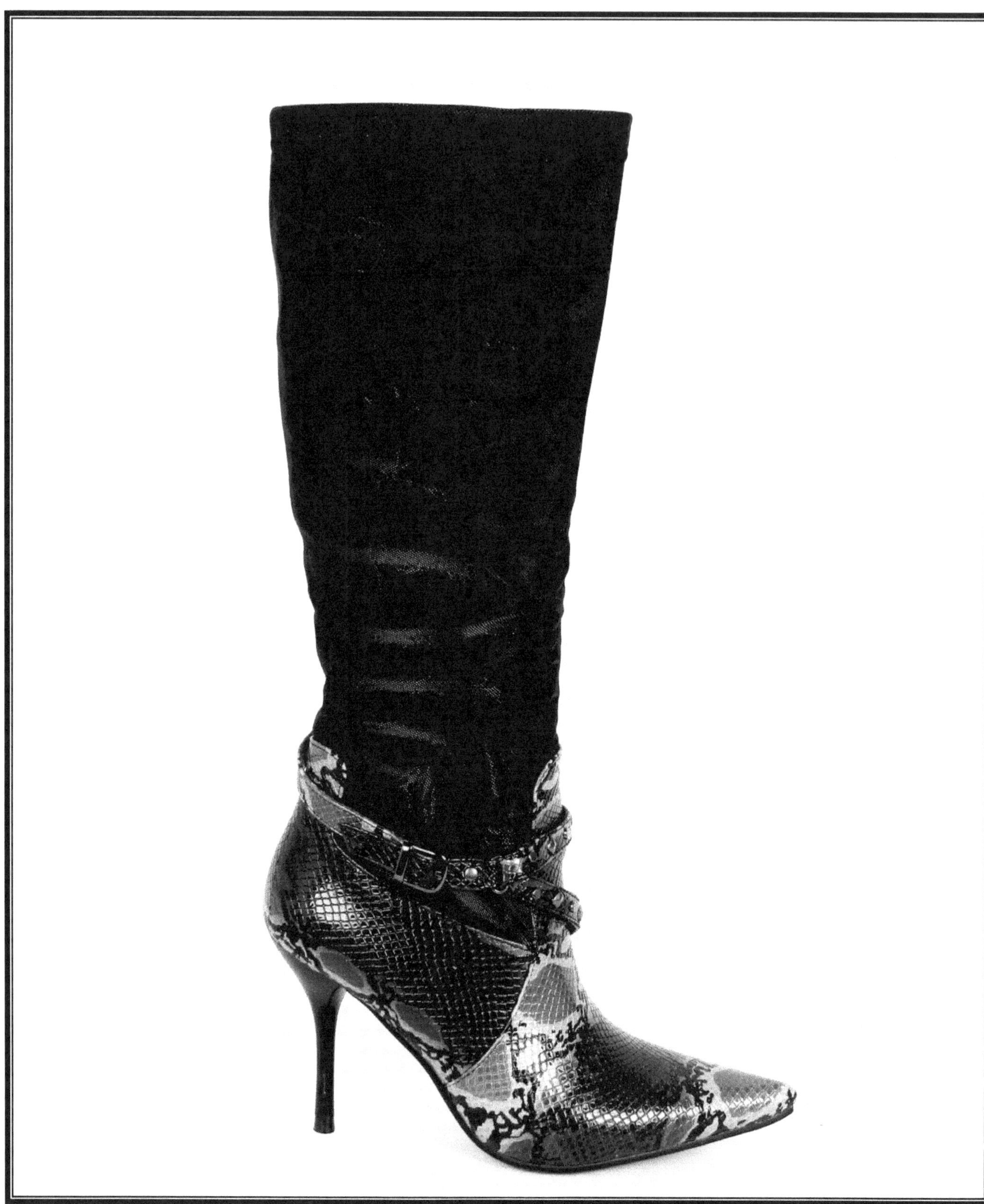

I Am A Blessed Woman Of God

I am a blessed woman of God
Woman of many shades
I demonstrate power through prayer
A blessed woman of God
I'm a star in Christ
He sacrifice his life,
For my sins
A blessed woman of God
Comfortable in, her own skin

I derive out of the North Philly streets
Yea, a black sister in the hood
My unusual characteristics
Was always miss understood
Should they have known?
That I am blessed woman of God
Held captive by Jesus Christ
My life is not my own
I was brought with a price
I will give birth at the appointed time
And when I do it will blow their minds
My prayers go through
I know God smiles down on me
Whispering, my child I will bless you
I speak with power
Cause the Holy Spirit lives in me.
I have too much dignity
Too allow Satan to devour me
I am a blessed women of God
Different and unique
Never meant to be like any of you
Living in His truth
I AM a blessed woman of God
A smile that goes a long way
Brighten up anybody's day
Eyes filled with wisdom
I'm blessed from
My clothes down to my shoes
I am a blessed woman of God

Its nothing, I did
Only what He did
His blood was smear
So I can have a second chance
This time! I am going to take life
In the palm of my hands
Meaning living life
Is actually dying for Christ
Some doors will open some will close to.
It's up to me not to sit home
Crying why I'm going through blues
I can do all things
Through Christ that's strengthens me
I am, blessed woman of God
Everybody is welcome to join me in this Holy Ghost party and praise thee

God knew me before the essence of the earth
He knew me before my Mother's birth
Before he made the grass, trees and the birds
I am a blessed woman of God
My voice shall be heard

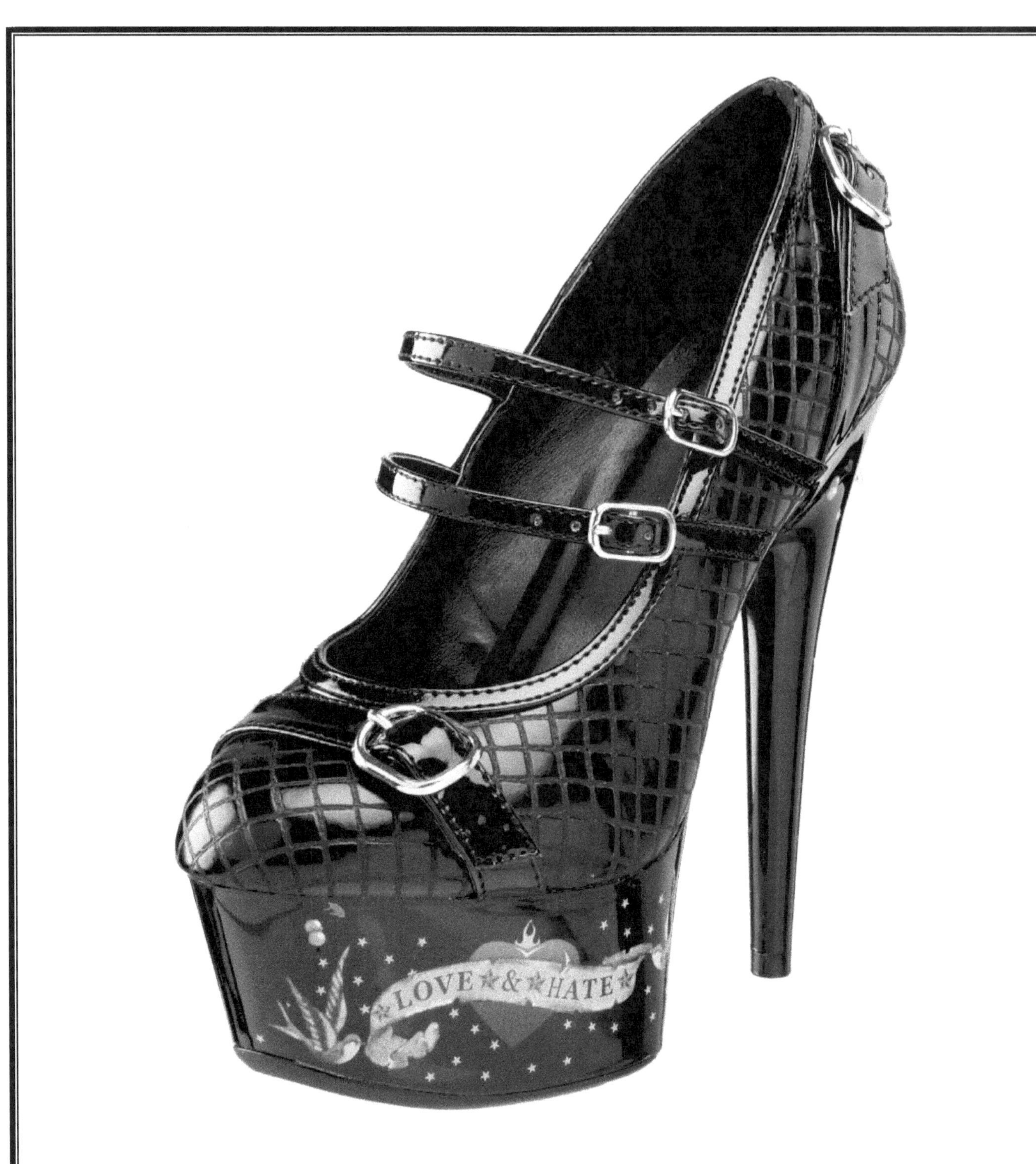
LOVE & HATE

Brain Damage

Brain Damage
I feel bewildered
Stuck between two worlds
As I go through
The battle of the mind
Going through the motions
Passing me by is time

Sitting back to contemplate
Things I would like to do
Don't want to think
Of the consequences
Of my actions once, I go through

I have brain damage
One not able to control or manage
The thoughts' running through my head
Satan playing tricks
By him I was being misled

Feeling guilty about my past
And what I did
Brain Damage
Stuck in a place of make believe & fantasies
Can't find my way back to reality
Wanting what I like
Even when it's wrong

Brain Damage
Sets you apart
Thinking wicked thoughts
In the dark

Brain damage
No therapist can fix
Giving into things
Merely to exist

Get your mind right
On Christ
You were bought
With a price

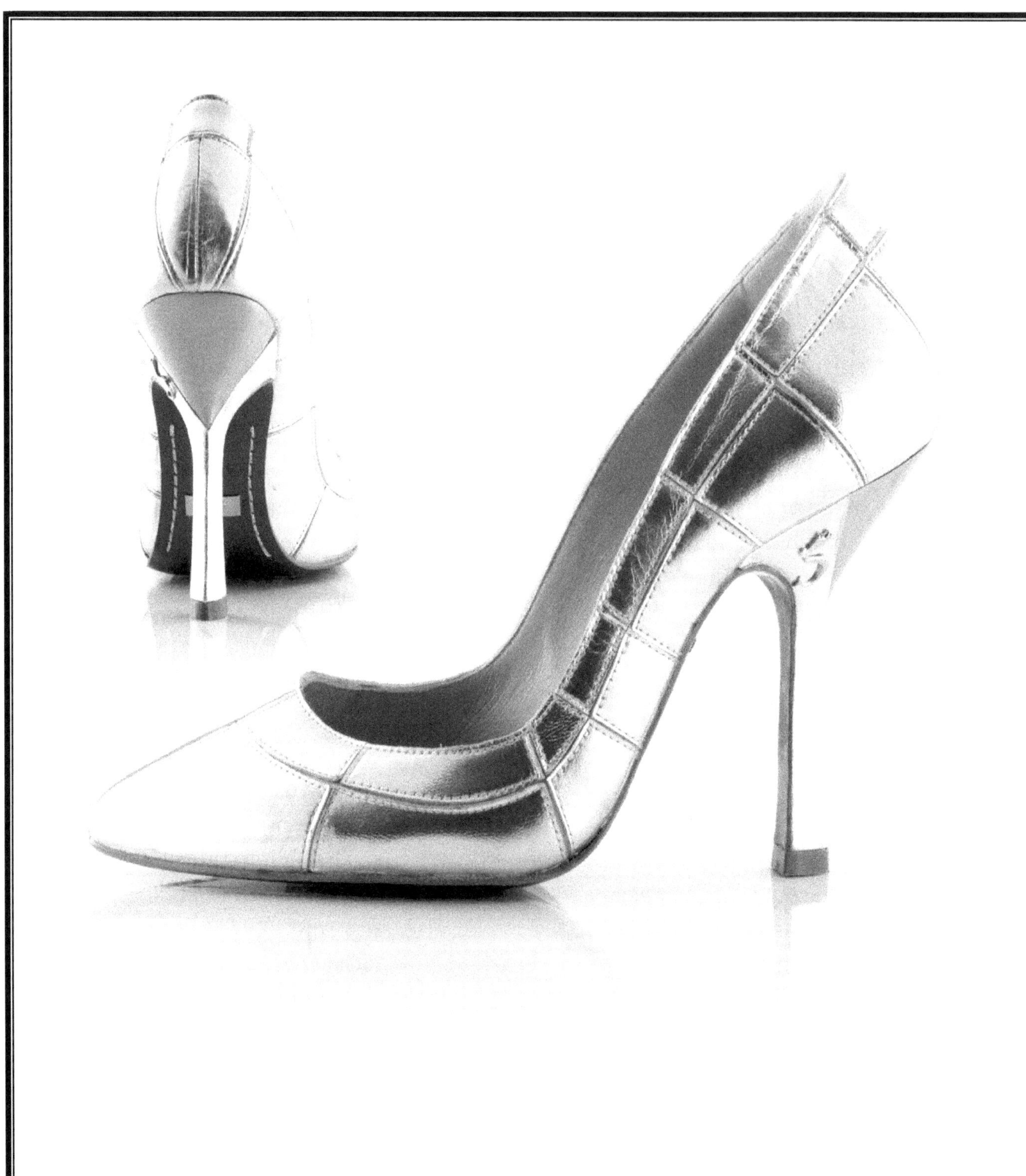

Blind Date

One day
Out of the blue
I get a phone call
On the other end, I heard,
"Girl guess who?
I have someone I want you to meet."

"Oh no" I replied
"Not a blind date
I'm not even dressed
Just let me go back to sleep."

She said, "This guy doesn't care how you look;
Just come as you are."

I said,
"Girl you gone too far
She said,
"Get cleaned up and come now!"

I gave her many excuses
But, she wouldn't come around
I asked, what man
Could be right for me?

She said "You'll see."

"Alright I'm on my way
This might be good
I was in all day"
I noticed I was in front of a Church
I yelled,
"Girl you lied!"

As I walked in
I heard the Pastor say that Jesus died
For our sins so we can live
Someone looked my way and ask,
"Are you born again?"

I said,
"No, I don't quite understand Jesus
Who is this man?"

"Go up in front"
My girlfriend said.

"Give Him a try
Ask him to come into your heart
He will change your life
Like He did mine"

I went up front scared, didn't know what to do
The Pastor took my hand and
Said,
"Jesus loves you."
I said,
"Lord please forgive me for all my sins
Come into my heart so I can be born again."

The next morning, I got up to pray
To thank God; for another day
When I arrived at work
I was running a little late
My co worker asked,
"Why are you so happy?"

I said,
"Last night I had a blind date."
She said,
"Girl, please tell me about this guy!"

I said,

"His name is Jesus, you should meet him
Just give him a try."

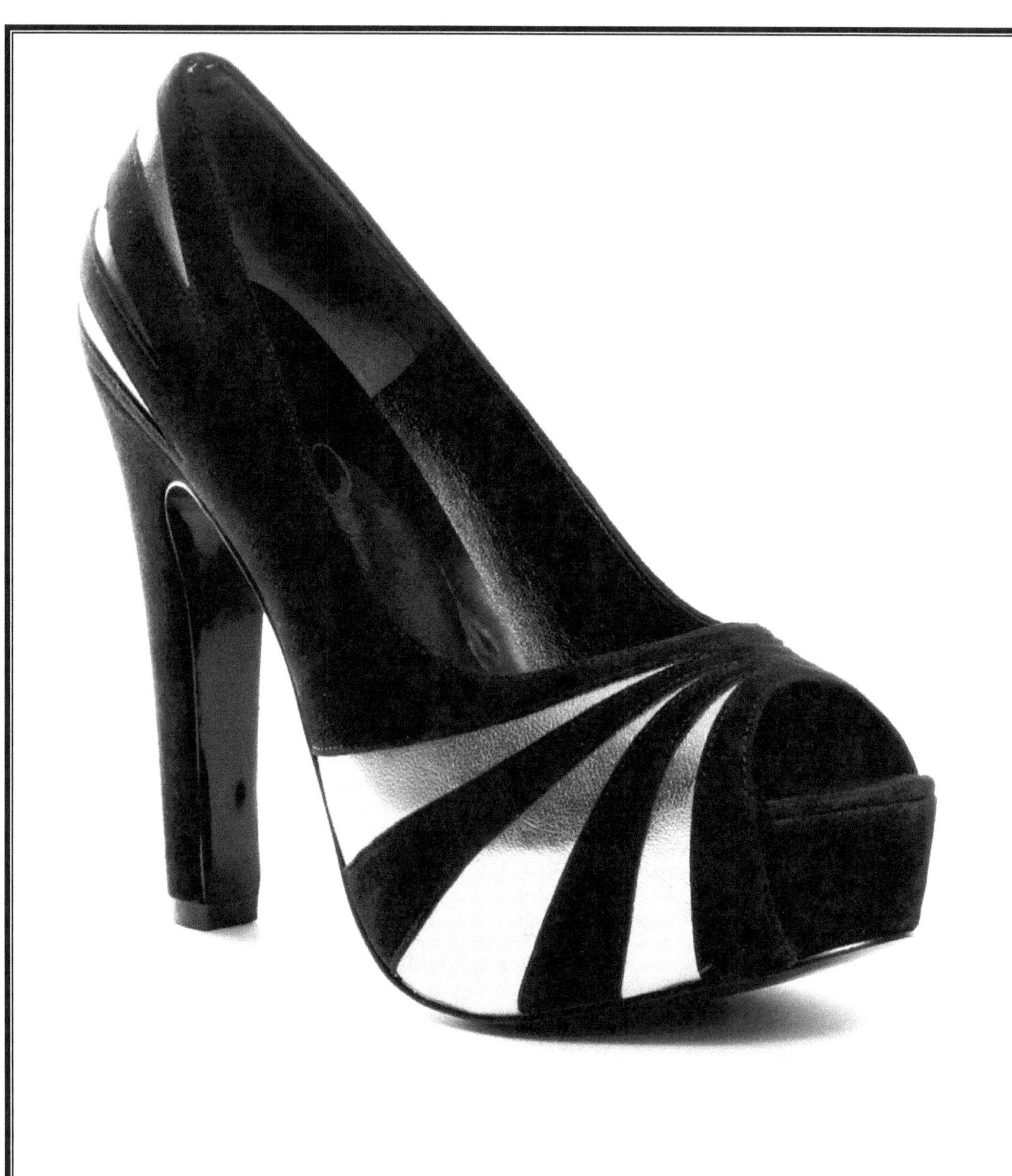

Have You?

Have you felt like giving up?
To the point
You can't go on
You felt so bound
Like a lion in a cage
Without a roar
Like an eagle about to fly
But, you realized you have no wings
Like a vocalists,
That lost their ability to sing
Have you ever; felt like a writer without a pen?
What about like the devil;
With no one to sin
Have you,
Felt like a song;
That lost its melody?
Have you,
Felt like giving up?
Needed to be set free.

Have you, felt like dry land
Where there is no rain?
Like the crack head, without the cocaine
Have you,
Felt like the schizophrenic without the sane?
Have you,
Ever felt you were on a job
With no pay?
Have you felt like going to church, without the Sunday?
Like a speaker,
With nothing to say
Have you,
Ever felt like a morning
Without the day?
Like a child,
Who lost theirs since of play
Have you,
Felt like a Christian
Who forgot how to pray?
I have; I felt this way

Have you, ever been sick,
And couldn't get well?
Had a story,
And no one to tell
Have you, ever been to the doctor and
They couldn't say,
What's wrong?
Have you, ever felt like you
Just didn't belong?
Have you ever felt like
You were,
At a wedding with no groom
Or fire,
With nothing to consume
Have you,
Ever felt pregnant and couldn't give birth?
Or, like a diamond that
Lost its worth.
I have; I felt this way

But,
I learned
Theirs no,
Testimony without the test
Theirs no,
Message without the mess
Theirs no,
Christ without the Cross.
Why preach the good news,
If no one were lost?
No anointing without the price
Do you feel like a gambler
Without the dice?
Theirs no,
Glory without the pain.
You must have the storm
If you want the rain

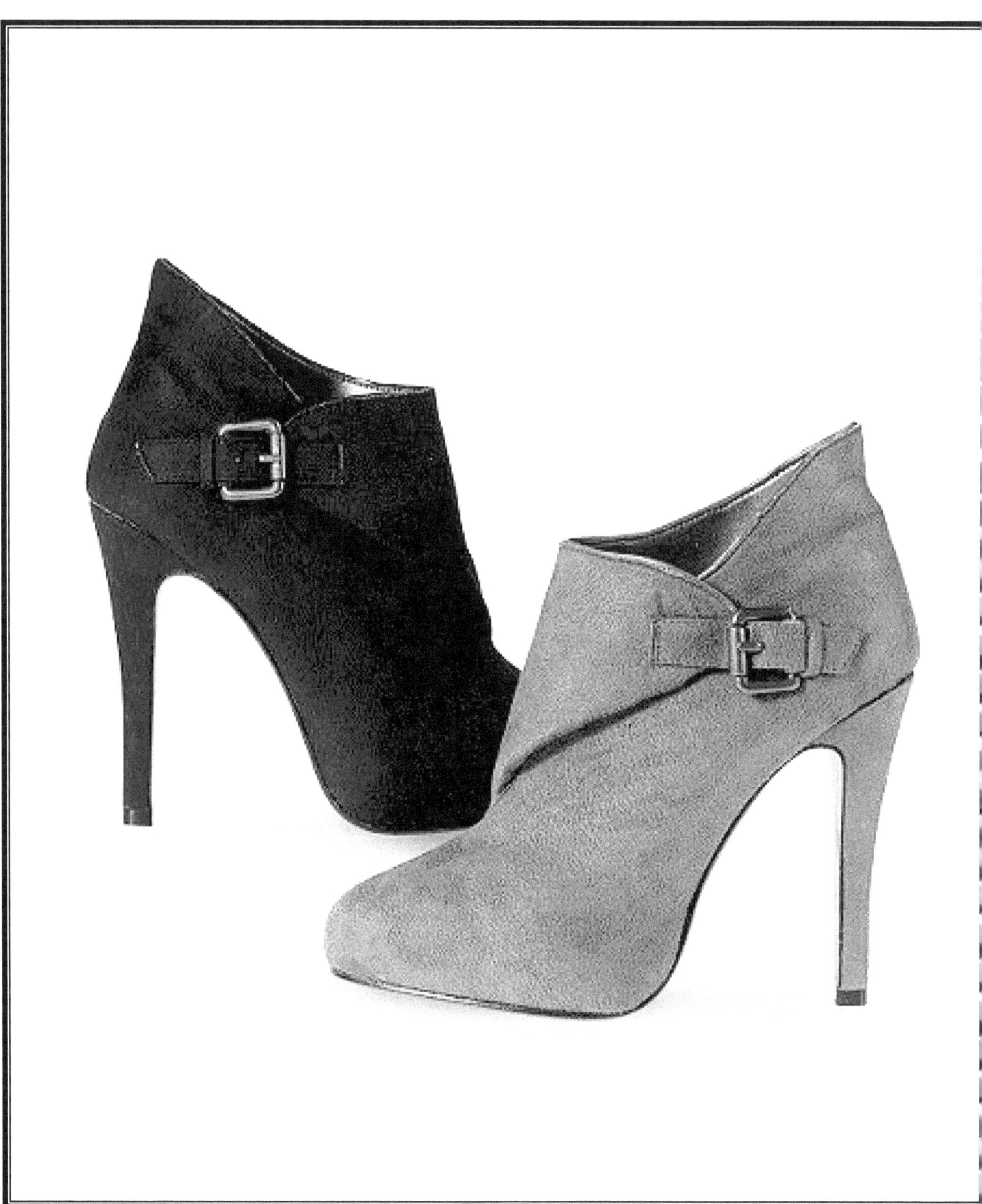

Strange Love

Must be strange for some to believe, how I could be in love with a man I can't see?

My friends argued,
Girl! It don't take all that
But, it's hard for me to
stay away
Like the rich,
With their money
If I want to be funny
Like a ladies man,
Smacking his woman
On the behind calling her
honey
Like a cop,
With his gun
Or a mother's love
With her new born son
Can't turn, my faith into
doubt
They rather go out
But, Instead
I'm home to pray
They don't understand
How my life changed
When we met on that
Sunday
I can't keep,
A man anymore
Because,
He's always competing
If, I'm not with him
He thinks I'm cheating
Because, most of my time
Is spent with him
I'm doing all I can,
To convey the truth
How my heart melted
Like a woman, that laid
eyes,
On a new pair of shoes,
Ooh
Time stands still, in his
presence
Is more than a cheap
thrill
That a mortal man can
fulfill
In the moment, of
unconditional love
Enjoying his embrace
They think it's strange
That preferably
I'm home to gaze in his
face
Must be strange for
some to believe
How I could be in love
with a man I can't see
The folks, on the outside
looking in
I must look derange
I know, I know, I got so
thin
My appetite hasn't been
the same since
I fell in love with him
We been meeting up, for
a while
You ask who this man is.
I just smile
Hard to utter the words,
How I been awakened
He's a risk worth taken
Others caused me pain
To the unbelievers I look
insane
Had many lovers and one
night stands
But, He wanted more,
Than what's in my pants
Heart was cold
I forgot how to feel love
again
Never have I met a man
That could love me in
spite of my sins
Hooked...
Do I looked delusional
talking to him
When you see no one
there
He hears me,
Even if he doesn't talk
back
It's a fact
Words not said, speaks
volume
So with that
It's unusual
To fall in love, with
someone
I hardly know
He loved me on the low
Some find it hard to
believe
That this love exists
It's like air,
I can't see it
But I know it's there
It's like gravity a scientific
fact
Like a love song
That plays in my head
It's still hard for some to
believe
How I could be in love
with a man I can't see
What if I am crazy?
Should I care what others
think?
About me seeing a shrink
It's really not that hard to
believe
It by faith, I don't need to
see
To be in love with
The man who saved me!

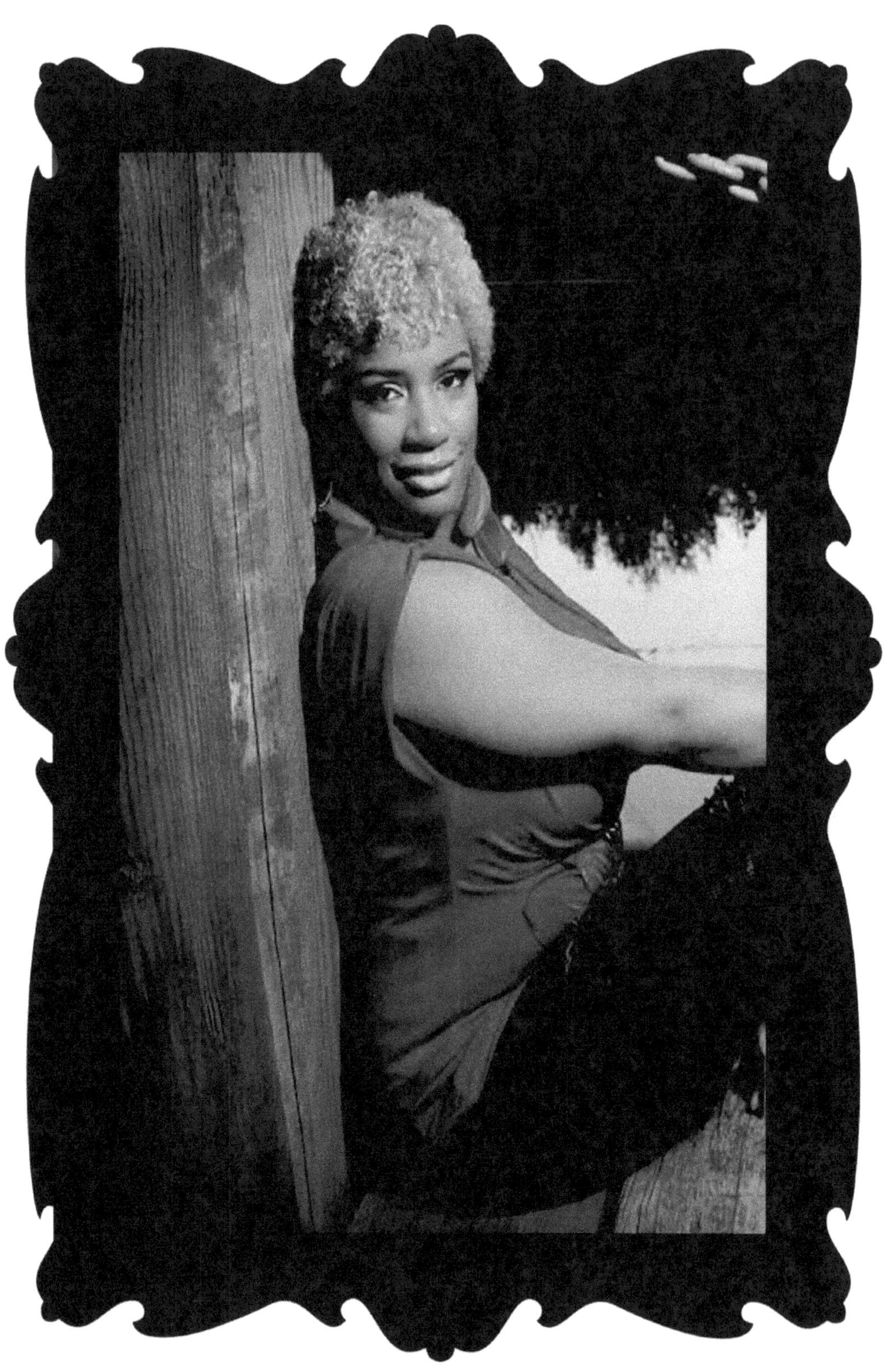

Can't Give Up on My Dreams

If I shoot for the stars
I may ascend upon the moon
Not now,
But soon,
Things will change
Faith is the exchange
For my dreams to come true

Reliance makes anything
believable
And my dreams achievable

My dreams are well overdue
I will not depart this life
Until they all come true

Have you wondered?
How and when will it come to
pass?
With the hindrance in your life
How long, will the struggle last?

Living,
Pay check to pay check
Working over time
To make ends meet
In the mid-night hour
I'm pacing the floor
Because my dreams won't let me
sleep

Working for a boss who despise
me
Cut my pay when I'm late
In the late night hour
I'm pacing the floor
Because the bills I owe
Keeps me awake
The closer I get to accomplish
my dreams
The harder it seems
For them to come true

When the storms in life
Seems too much to bear
Hold your dreams near
Can't give up on my dreams
I need to believe

When my friends don't
understand
Against all odds
I have to stand
Push through obstacles

Have no where to turn
Gone through the fire
Came out without many burns
I can't give up on my dreams
I need to believe.

Giving up on my dreams,
Is like
The women who aborted
Her baby she never knew
Giving up on my dreams,
Is like
The homeless
Without a home

Giving up on my dreams,
Is like
The Insane who
Can't perceive what's true
Giving up on my dreams
Is like
Owing a bill that's over due
Giving up on my dreams
Is like
A marriage that lost the sense of
anew
Giving up on my dreams
Is like
A church with empty pews
So you see,
I can't give up on my dreams
I need to believe

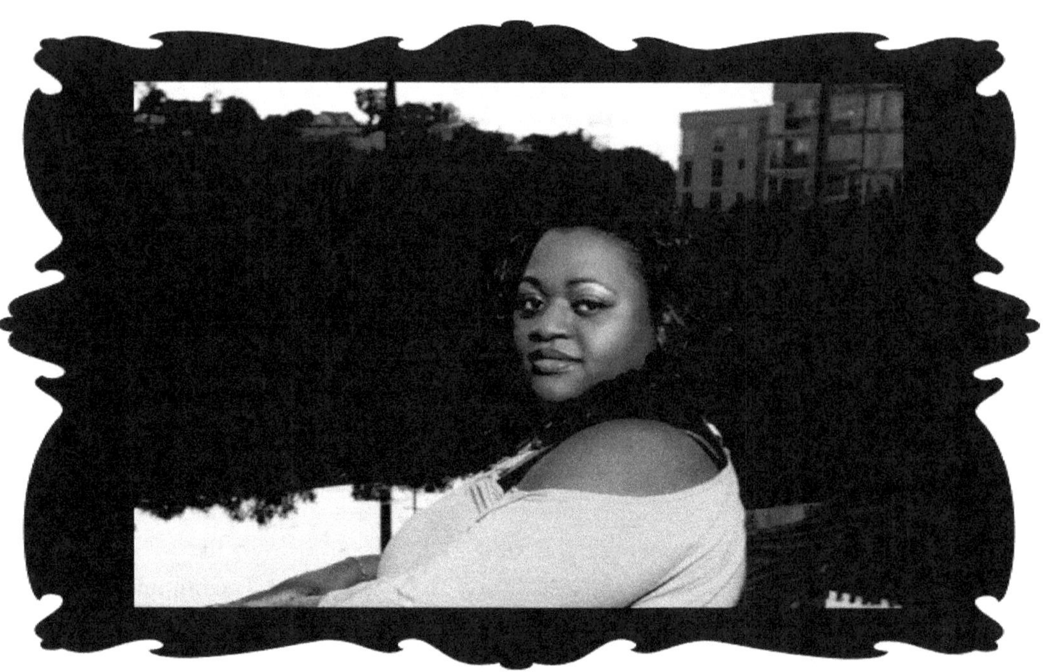

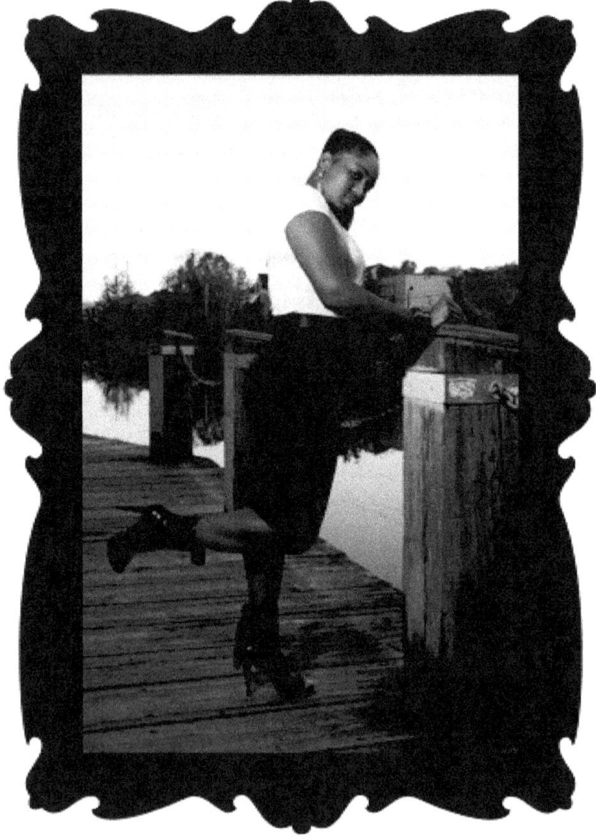

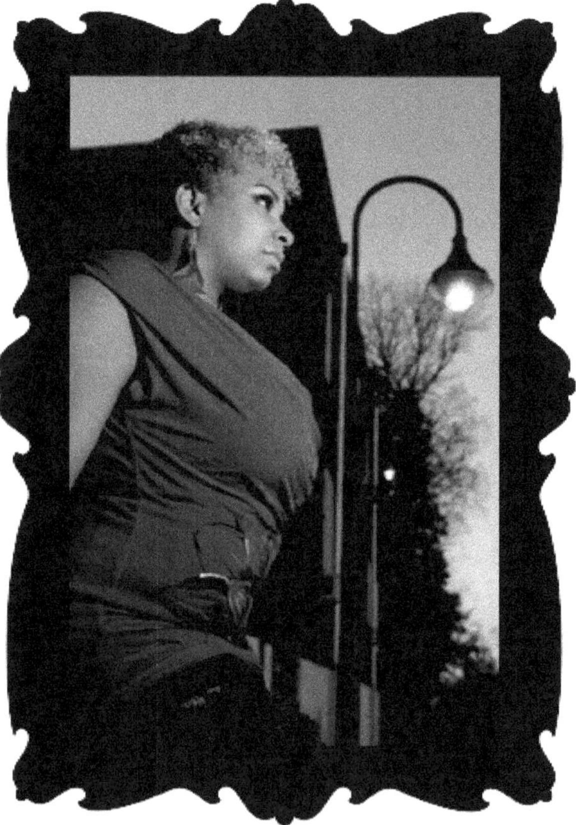

Thank You

Glory to God for all of our gifts!

We thank all of our family and friends for their support along our journey. Love and support of those connected to us give us the strength that we need to travel our destined path in life.

To Our Readers: We salute you! Without your interest in our craft we would merely be writing for sport. Our words would never be able to reach the eyes, ears and hearts of others...Thanks for reading our souls.

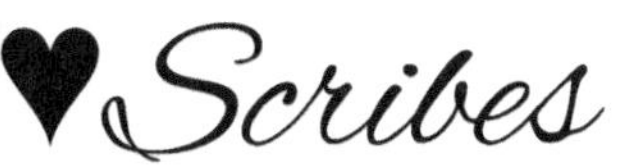

www.ingramcontent.com/pod-product-compliance
Lightning Source LLC
LaVergne TN
LVHW061248100826
845148LV00008B/1061